The Music Theory Handbook

Marjorie Merryman

Boston University School for the Arts

HARCOURT BRACE COLLEGE PUBLISHERS

Fort Worth • Philadelphia • San Diego • New York • Orlando • Austin • San Antonio

Toronto • Montreal • London • Sydney • Tokyo

Publisher	CHRISTOPHER P. KLEIN
Acquisitions Editor	BARBARA J. C. ROSENBERG
Developmental Editor	J. CLAIRE BRANTLEY
Project Editor	JEFF BECKHAM
Production Manager	DEBRA A. JENKIN
Art Director	BURL DEAN SLOAN

ISBN: 0-15-502662-3

Library of Congress Catalog Card Number: 96-76368

Requests for permission to make copies of any part of the work should be mailed to: Permissions Department, Harcourt Brace & Company, 6277 Sea Harbor Drive, Orlando, Florida 32887-6777.

Address for Editorial Correspondence: Harcourt Brace College Publishers, 301 Commerce Street, Suite 3700, Fort Worth, TX 76102.

Address for Orders: Harcourt Brace & Company, 6277 Sea Harbor Drive, Orlando, FL 32887-6777. 1-800-782-4479, or 1-800-433-0001 (in Florida).

Harcourt Brace College Publishers may provide complimentary instructional aids and supplements or supplement packages to those adopters qualified under our adoption policy. Please contact your sales representative for more information. If as an adopter or potential user you receive supplements you do not need, please return them to your sales representative or send them to:

Attn: Returns Department
Troy Warehouse
465 South Lincoln Drive
Troy, MO 63379

This book was printed on recycled paper made from 10% post-consumer waste and 40% pre-consumer waste. The total recycled fiber content is 50% by fiber weight.

Printed in the United States of America

6 7 8 9 0 1 2 3 4 5 053 10 9 8 7 6 5 4 3 2 1

PREFACE

The purpose of this *Music Theory Handbook* is to provide a clear background text for college-level study of music theory. The text is extremely concise and is meant to support the lectures, exercises, and analysis that take place in a theory class. Much of the information is technical in nature because it is designed to reinforce and clarify, like a good set of class notes, the techniques and mechanics involved in such topics as notation, counterpoint, and voice-leading.

Students may wonder what the purpose is of learning "rules" of harmony and counterpoint. Isn't music a creative art? The answer to these questions lies in the nature of theory itself, and in its relationship to musical literature. The theory contained in this book relates primarily to the common practice period (roughly 1700–1900), during which time composers shared, in general terms, fundamental assumptions about the workings of harmony and counterpoint. The "rules" of harmony and counterpoint are drawn not from abstract theories, but from the general practice of these composers across a span of more than two hundred years. With this technical background, students can understand the bulk of the music they hear, play, and sing in concerts, in orchestra, chorus, in recitals and chamber music and so on. Students may use these techniques as the basis for creating new works in the styles of Bach, Mozart, Beethoven, and Brahms. Work of this sort develops the ear, since stylistic refinements require a detailed hearing. Creative students will also use these technical studies as a jumping-off point for original work that is not bound by common practice "rules," but which shows a sophisticated awareness of our musical past. This is, in fact the common ground shared by most composers of the twentieth century.

No book can do the work of music literature in the study of this subject. The text here is generally not accompanied by fragments of musical examples from the literature, because such examples rarely mean anything outside of their larger contexts, and tend to be ignored by students. It is therefore essential that this book be used in conjunction with analysis of appropriate pieces. An excellent source for such examples is the *Anthology for Musical Analysis,* edited by Charles Burkhart. Several other good anthologies are also available.

The text does, of course, contain basic musical examples, and these should be played as the material is read. In Part 7 of this book are keyboard exercises that are designed to reinforce aurally the technical studies contained in the text. Part 8 provides exercises that are keyed to the material introduced in Parts 1–4. Because the text is concise, curious students may wish to know of other, more specialized books on some of the subjects contained here. To facilitate this, there is a brief listing of suggested further reading at the end of each part of the text.

This book has been used at Boston University for undergraduate music majors (freshman, sophomore, and junior theory) as well as for graduate theory review. The different sections are fairly self-contained so that they may be studied, skimmed or skipped, according to the needs of the particular course. If, for example, this book is used in a course that skips species counterpoint, students will find that essential information, such as definitions of non-harmonic tones, is also contained in the unit on harmony.

I would like to thank all the many colleagues and students who have given time, energy, and excellent suggestions, and I would like especially to thank my husband, composer Edward Cohen, for advice, patience, and affectionate encouragement.

CONTENTS

PART 1

Fundamentals

CLEFS, GRAND STAFF, KEY SIGNATURES

The five-line grid on which music is written is called the **staff** (plural—
staffs or *staves*). Two or more staffs braced together are often called a **system.** At the beginning of each line of music, each staff needs to have a clef
and key signature. At the beginning of a new piece (or an exercise) each
staff needs also to have a time signature, but the time signature is not
repeated on subsequent systems. A discussion of time signatures, rhythmic
notation, and alignment can be found under the heading "Rhythm and
Meter," below.

Clefs

The **clefs** commonly seen in music today are **treble, bass, alto,** and **tenor.**
The example shows each clef with a middle C. The treble clef is also called
the G-clef, because its spiral center identifies the pitch G (above middle C).
The bass clef is also called the F-clef, because its two dots identify the pitch
F (below middle C). Alto and tenor clefs are called **C-clefs,** because the
center of the clef sign always indicates middle C. The other C-clefs shown
below are mainly encountered in old editions of preclassical music. As with
alto and tenor clefs, the center of the clef sign is middle C. The purpose of
the various clefs is notational convenience: music can be written in various
registers without too many ledger lines. **Ledger lines** are the small lines
that extend the staff up or down, as can be seen in treble and bass clefs
below.

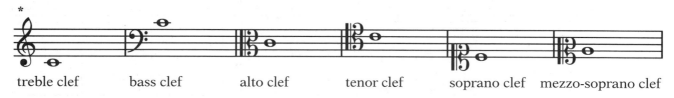

treble clef   bass clef   alto clef   tenor clef   soprano clef   mezzo-soprano clef

Grand Staff

A bracing together of treble and bass clef staves
is called a **grand staff.** This is the familiar format
of most keyboard music. Middle C appears in the
middle of the grand staff in both treble and bass
clefs, but notice that the placement of ledger
lines makes a clear distinction between middle C
in the treble clef and middle C in the bass clef.

---

* all show middle c

1

Clefs identify specific pitches; in the example above, the C shown is not *any* pitch C, it is middle C. If we go to the piano and start at middle C, we can play eight successive ascending white notes: C, D, E, F, G, A, B, and C. The distance between middle C and the seventh white note above it, also called C, is an **octave.** Tones that are an octave apart sound similar, but not exactly the same, because one is higher and one is lower. The location of a pitch in terms of high and low is its **register.** Pitches of the same name but in different registers are called **octave equivalents.** In Western music, the idea of octave equivalence is very important, and is so much a part of everyday musical experience that we tend to take it for granted.

Musical notation is precise as to the *register* of each pitch. In writing about music, we may mean to identify a pitch, but not a particular register. A pitch of nonspecific register is often called a **pitchclass.** Specifying a particular pitch in a precise register can be quite cumbersome in prose. For example, we might want to call attention to the C that is two octaves above middle C (example 1), or to the F that is below the C below middle C (example 2).

A system has been developed to solve the problem of naming specific pitches in register. In this system, middle C is designated c^1, called "one-line C." The first white note above c^1 is called d^1, then e^1, and so on up to the next C, which is designated as c^2 ("two-line C"). The pitch two octaves higher than c^1 is c^3 ("three-line C") and so on. Below c^1 is c ("small C"), then C ("great C"), then C_1 (or CC, called "contra C") and C_2 (or CCC, called "subcontra C"). All the other pitches can be named in accordance with the C they lie directly above, as shown in the next example.

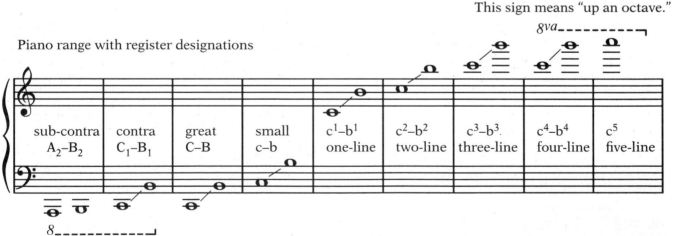

Piano range with register designations

This sign means "up an octave."

This sign means "down an octave."

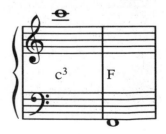

Now we can see that the pitch in example 1 is c^3 ("three-line C") and example 2 is F ("great F").

This system is well known, but is not universally used. In this book, we will use *uppercase letters to name major keys* (C major, F major), and *lowercase letters will signify minor keys* (c minor, f minor). To avoid confusion, this book does not make use of the pitch/register method outlined above. It is included here for reference and for familiarity, since it is widely used in analytic writing.

Keys and Key Signatures

Key is a crucial organizing idea of Western music of the seventeenth, eighteenth, and nineteenth centuries. When we say that a piece of music is in a given key (C major, for example), we mean that the pitch-class C will serve as a goal of motion and a point of repose; we mean that all the pitches used in the piece somehow ultimately support C as the central, organizing force; we mean that the melodic and harmonic material of the piece is derived, on some level, from the C-major scale. Topics hinted at here (scales, harmonies, functions, and relationships of notes within a key) will be taken up later. First it will be helpful simply to learn the key signatures. These should be memorized.

The chart shows key signatures for all major and minor keys (a discussion of the difference between major and minor scales and keys follows). Observe that as each sharp is added, the key rises by five consecutive letter names (C-D-E-F-G; G-A-B-C-D; and so on). The sharps themselves are also added in an order rising successively by five note-names. As flats are added, the pattern of keys descends (goes backwards) by five consecutive letters (F-E-D-C-B and so on). In addition, the flats themselves form a pattern of successive descending fifths. These patterns form the **circle of fifths.**

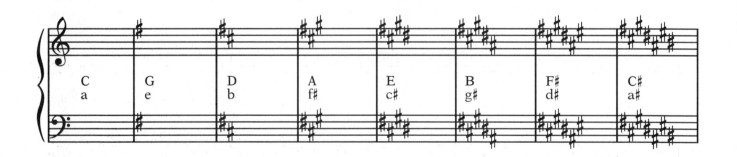

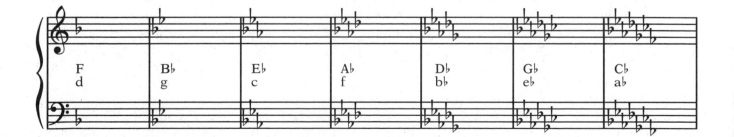

Circle of Fifths

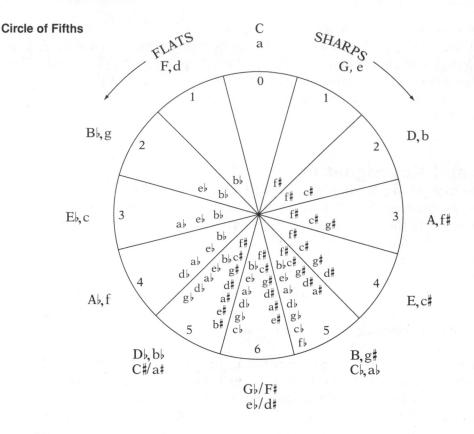

Major and minor keys that share the same key signature are *relatives*. Every major key has a **relative minor,** and every minor key has a **relative major.** The relative minor key begins three letter-names below its relative major, and the relative major key begins three letter-names above its relative minor. Relatives are shown on the chart above and on the circle of fifths.

SCALES AND MODES

At the keyboard, find the pitch C. Starting on C, play eight adjacent white notes rising in pitch (C-D-E-F-G-A-B-C). This is the **C-major scale,** a specific pattern of pitch relationships. In conventional Western music, all scales are patterns made up almost entirely of **half steps** and **whole steps,** with the half step defined as the smallest possible distance between two notes (this is the distance between adjacent keys on the keyboard or adjacent frets on the guitar). A half-step can also be called a **semitone.** B to C, D to E-flat, E to F are half steps. A whole step is equivalent to two half steps. B-flat to C, C to D, E to F-sharp are whole steps. When we play the C-major scale, we are playing this pattern: whole step, whole step, half step, whole step, whole step, whole step, half step. This pattern can be moved (*transposed*) to start from *any* note on the keyboard.

The examples below show first the major and minor scales. Half steps are indicated, as are any steps larger than a whole step (only the harmonic minor scale and pentatonic scale contain steps larger than the whole step). All other (unmarked) steps are whole steps.

Major Scale

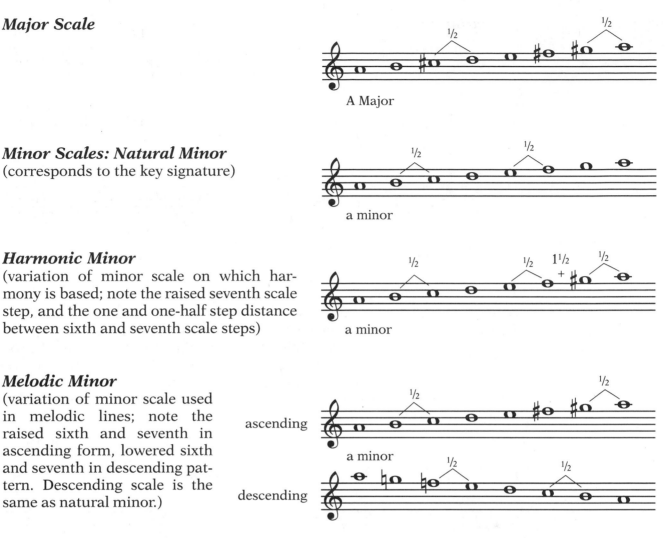

A Major

Minor Scales: Natural Minor
(corresponds to the key signature)

a minor

Harmonic Minor
(variation of minor scale on which harmony is based; note the raised seventh scale step, and the one and one-half step distance between sixth and seventh scale steps)

a minor

Melodic Minor
(variation of minor scale used in melodic lines; note the raised sixth and seventh in ascending form, lowered sixth and seventh in descending pattern. Descending scale is the same as natural minor.)

ascending

a minor

descending

Chromatic Scale
(this scale consists entirely of half steps)

   Scale patterns other than major, minor, and chromatic have been commonly used in early music (i.e., before 1730) and in late nineteenth- or twentieth-century music. The three scales given below are found in Western music of the nineteenth and twentieth centuries, and also in non-Western music. Following these is a brief explanation and listing of the church modes, which were the building blocks of European music in medieval and renaissance times.

Whole Tone Scale (all whole steps)

Pentatonic Scale

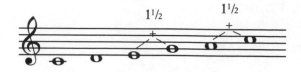

Octatonic Scale (alternates whole and half steps, can start with either)

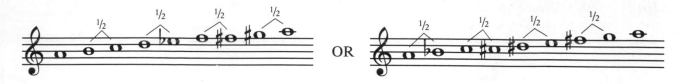

OR

Church Modes

The church modes are not completely analogous to scales in tonal music. Each mode implies not only a succession of steps, but also specific cadence (ending) points and characteristic melodic fragments and conventions. Each mode has a specific cadence pitch (final) as well as a secondary pitch center (dominant). Each mode also has a specific range (ambitus). In so-called "authentic" modes, the ambitus is generally tonic to the octave above. Plagal modes (all designated by the prefix *hypo-*) are based on authentic modes, but range from the fourth below the final to the fifth above it.

$\widehat{o}$ = final   o = dominant

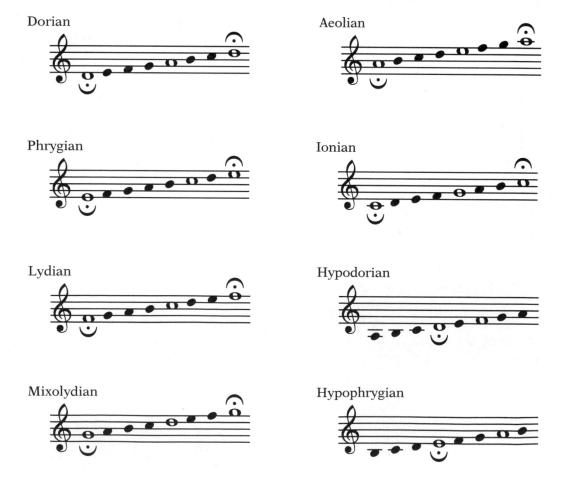

Dorian

Aeolian

Phrygian

Ionian

Lydian

Hypodorian

Mixolydian

Hypophrygian

Hypolydian

Hypoaeolian

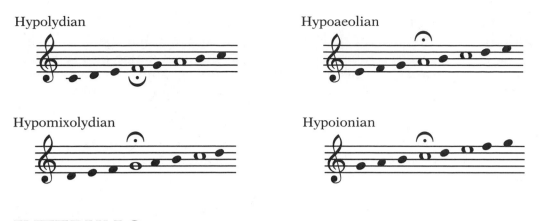

Hypomixolydian

Hypoionian

INTERVALS

An **interval** is the distance between two pitches. We call this an interval whether the pitches are presented simultaneously, or one after the other. The conventions for naming and counting intervals are closely tied to tonal music and scale patterns. Major and minor scales always contain notes in an unbroken succession of letter-names, and intervals are classified as **seconds, thirds, fourths, fifths, sixths,** and **sevenths** by counting from one letter-name to another. Thus, a up to b is a second, a up to c (a-b-c) is a third, a up to d (a-b-c-d) is a fourth, and so on. To think in terms of downward intervals, we count backwards through the letter-names. From g down to f is a second, g down to e (g-f-e) is a third, g down to c (g-f-e-d-c) is a fifth, g down to a (g-f-e-d-c-b-a) is a seventh. An **octave** is the interval from a pitch of a given letter-name to a pitch with the same name in a different register. A **unison** is the interval formed by pitches with the same letter-name in the same register.

By convention, *intervals of seconds, thirds, sixths, and sevenths are described as major, minor, diminished, or augmented.* Unisons, fourths, fifths, and octaves are referred to as perfect, diminished, or augmented. The following example shows major, minor, and perfect intervals ascending from the pitch A (m = minor; M = major; P = perfect).

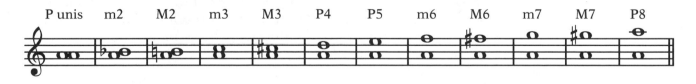

The next example shows major, minor, and perfect intervals *descending* from A.

Note that only seconds, thirds, sixths, and sevenths can be major or minor. Only octaves, fourths, and fifths are perfect. There is no such thing as a perfect third, a major fifth, a perfect second, or a minor fourth.

An interval that is a semitone (half step) smaller than minor is called **diminished.** An interval that is a semitone smaller than perfect is also called diminished. An interval a semitone larger than major, or a semitone larger than perfect, is called **augmented.** See the example below for some augmented and diminished intervals from the pitch A (d = diminished; A = augmented; dd = doubly diminished). Intervals of augmented fourth and of diminished fifth are also called **tritones.**

Doubly diminished means a semitone smaller than diminished. **Doubly augmented** means a semitone larger than augmented. See the example below.

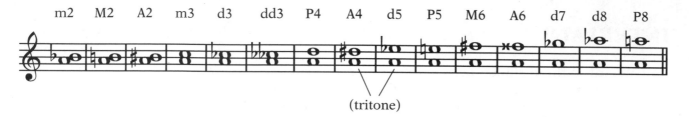

For most people, the easiest way to count intervals is by comparing them to scale patterns. In the example below, observe that all the major intervals belong to the A-major scale. Except for the minor second, the A-minor (natural minor) scale includes all the minor intervals. The perfect intervals belong to both major and minor scales.

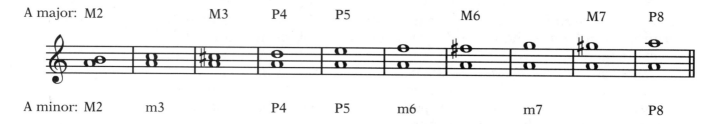

What about intervals *descending* from a given note? The example below compares descending intervals to the A-major and A-minor descending scales. The descending major scale produces all the minor intervals, while the descending natural minor scale produces all the major intervals except for the major seventh. Once again, the perfect intervals belong to both major and minor scales.

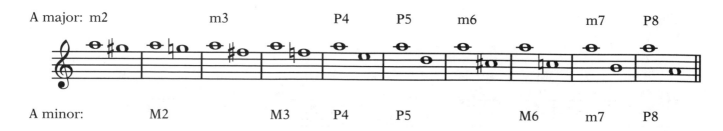

In order to become proficient in naming and recognizing intervals, it is necessary to know all major and minor scales.

There are other ways of counting intervals. One way is to count the half steps: A to B♭ = one half step = a minor second. A to B♮ = two half steps

= a major second, etc. The method of naming intervals by counting half steps is logical and is frequently used in contemporary music and analysis. The difficulty of this method lies in the fact that the number of half steps between two pitches does not tell us anything about the scale step or letter-names of the pitches. For example, the interval 6 represents the pitch that is six half steps away from the starting point. From A, this pitch could be spelled as D♯, or as E♭ (pitch names representing the same sounds with different spellings are called **enharmonic equivalents**). The interval 2 from A (the pitch that is two half steps up from A) could be spelled B♮, but it could also be spelled C♭ (enharmonic equivalents). In tonal music these are important distinctions, but in music not based on major or minor scales, enharmonic spellings may not have any significance, and integer designations for intervals can be very useful.

MAJOR AND MINOR SCALE DEGREES

In major and minor scales, *pitches are named in an unbroken succession of letters, with no gaps and no repeats* until the octave. A common confusion in spelling pitch names occurs when the succession of letter-names is violated. For example, in the key of C♯ major (C♯ D♯ E♯ F♯ G♯ A♯ B♯ C♯), the seventh scale step must be spelled B♯, not C♮. B♯ and C♮ are enharmonic equivalents, but only B♯ belongs to the key of C♯.

Scale Degrees

In tonal music, each scale degree (first note, second note, etc.) has a name, as shown below. Scale degrees are also referred to with Arabic numerals marked with a circumflex (^).

note in scale (scale step)	pitch in C major	scale degree name	scale degree number
first	C	**tonic**	$\hat{1}$
second	D	**supertonic**	$\hat{2}$
third	E	**mediant**	$\hat{3}$
fourth	F	**subdominant**	$\hat{4}$
fifth	G	**dominant**	$\hat{5}$
sixth	A	**submediant**	$\hat{6}$
seventh	B	**leading tone**[*]	$\hat{7}$
eighth	C	**tonic**	$\hat{8}$ or $\hat{1}$

These names for the scale degrees are used for major and minor scales, including the variants of the minor scales.

---

[*] In minor, if the seventh step is lowered, it is not a leading tone; it is often called the **subtonic, lowered seventh,** or **natural seventh.** The leading tone (raised seventh in minor) is always a half step below the tonic.

Note that major and minor are also referred to as modes, and that a change from major to minor keys of the same name (for example, from G major to g minor) is a **change of mode** rather than a change of key. Keys of the same name but different mode (G major and g minor) are called **parallel** (don't confuse this with **relative**—relative keys share the same key signature, for example, G major and e minor). Parallel keys share their tonic, supertonic, subdominant, dominant, and leading tone.

Functions and Tendency Tones

In the context of major and minor keys, some scale steps have particular functions or tendencies. These functions and tendencies create impressions of relative stability and instability that are extremely critical to the coherence of tonal music. This subject will come up again in the study of harmony, but for now, some purely melodic features can be appreciated. *The most stable element in the scale is the tonic.* A tune will sound more completed if it ends on the tonic note rather than on some other scale degree. The third scale step, and to a lesser extent the dominant, also have some melodic stability. *The least stable scale step is the leading tone.* This is a **tendency tone** not only because it is unstable, but because it suggests a particular continuation: The leading tone tends to move to the tonic. Another strong tendency tone is the *sixth scale step of the harmonic minor scale.* This note has a strong tendency to move down to the dominant. Other scale steps also have tendencies in relation to one another, but this will become much more clear when harmony is introduced.

The two tendency tones mentioned above, the leading tone and the lowered sixth, are important for understanding the variations of minor scales. In the melodic minor, the raised sixth and seventh scale steps carry the melodic line upwards, toward the upper tonic. Therefore, the raised sixth and seventh scale steps are part of the ascending melodic minor. The lowered seventh and sixth scale steps tend to carry the line down, toward the dominant. Thus the lowered seventh and sixth are part of the descending melodic minor.

RHYTHM AND METER

Meter refers to the underlying beat in music, and is almost always linked to the idea of a regular pattern of strong and weak beats. **Rhythm** refers to surface aspects of musical timing, including the length of notes and rests and the pattern of attacks. **Tempo** means the speed at which the music is performed. Rhythm may support the underlying meter, or may work against it, creating **syncopations** or **cross-accents** (see below). Music of a particular meter and rhythm may be performed at a variety of tempi.

Rhythmic values are organized around a simple system of equivalents, as follows:

whole = 2 half   = 4 quarter = 8 eighth notes   16 sixteenth notes   = × 32 = × 64
note   notes   notes   32 thirty-seconds =
                                                                                   64 sixty-fourths

A **dot** adds half the rhythmic value to any note or rest it follows. A *second dot* adds half of what the first dot added. Notes or rests with two dots are usually described as **double-dotted.** It is important to learn to recognize common patterns of dotted note values, such as:

Triplets, quintuplets, etc. generally squeeze more subdivisions of a given kind into a beat than it would ordinarily hold. Thus a quarter note = two eighths = three triplet eighths. A quarter = four sixteenths = five quintuplet sixteenths.

Time signatures consist of two numbers, one on top of the other. Avoid common notational errors such as writing the numbers side by side, or putting a line between the two numbers (time signatures are not fractions, even though *in prose* they are sometimes written 2/4, 3/4, etc., like fractions). A time signature should appear on all staves at the beginning of a piece. The time signature is not repeated on subsequent systems as the music goes on.

In all time signatures, the bottom number indicates a type of note as the unit of regularity (half note = 2, quarter note = 4, eighth note = 8, sixteenth note = 16, etc.). The upper number shows the number of these units per bar:

$\frac{4}{4}$ means 4 quarter-note units per bar.

$\frac{3}{8}$ means 3 eighth-note units per bar.

$\frac{7}{16}$ means 7 sixteenth-note units per bar.

Most meters in music may be divided into duple meters and triple meters. **Duple** meters are those meters based on even divisions of two and multiples of two, such as two-four, four-four, four-eight, etc. **Triple** meters are based on units of three, such as three-four and three-eight. These meters are also called **simple,** as in *simple duple* and *simple triple.* **Compound duple** meters are based on multiples of 2 × 3, such as six-eight and twelve-eight. **Compound triple** meters are based on multiples of 3 × 3, such as nine-eight. *Note the difference between three-four* (a triple) *and* *six-eight* (a compound duple): Each meter contains six eighth notes per bar, but a three-four meter divides those eighths into three quarter-note beats, while a six-eight meter divides them into two dotted-quarter beats.

In many harmonic and contrapuntal situations, a distinction must be made between *"strong" and "weak" beats*. In duple meters, the downbeat (first beat of the measure) is strongest, the odd-numbered beats are considered relatively strong, while the even-numbered beats are weak. In triple meters, the downbeat is strongest and the third beat is weakest. All off-beat units are weak.

Notation of rhythm generally reflects the metric divisions. This usually means showing strong beats, even if they are not sounded or attacked. In $\frac{4}{8}$, $\frac{6}{8}$, $\frac{12}{8}$ time (etc.), this means showing the second half of the measure as a strong beat. Internal strong beats do not need to be shown if the rhythm is a held note or a rest lasting an entire measure, and some simple off-beat rhythmic patterns are conventionally notated without showing strong beats. Good notational practice beams eighths, sixteenths, etc., together within beats, but not across strong beats.

The examples below show rhythmic patterns first incorrectly notated, and then corrected to correspond to the indicated meters. Note that in each case, the rhythmic values remain the same. Changing to correct notation makes the rhythm easier to read and more immediately reflective of the underlying accent pattern.

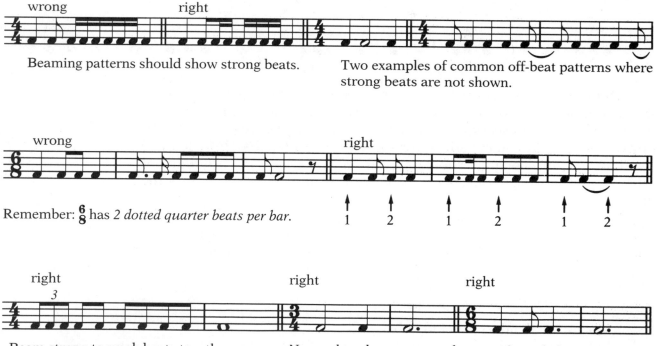

Beaming patterns should show strong beats.

Two examples of common off-beat patterns where strong beats are not shown.

Remember: $\frac{6}{8}$ has *2 dotted quarter beats per bar*.

Beam strong-to-weak beats together, but not where doing so causes confusion.

No need to show separate beats within whole measure units.

A **syncopation** is an accent on a weak beat or an off-beat. Patterns of repeating syncopations often form accompaniment figures or important motivic material. If a syncopation is quite simple or if it is repeated, it is likely to be notated as simply as possible, without showing strong beats in each bar.

Simple syncopation patterns need not show all strong beats.

A more complicated example showing all strong beats.

Cross-accents are syncopations that may suggest some meter other than the prevailing one. A **hemiola** uses cross-accents to establish a temporary sense of duple in a prevailing triple meter, or a temporary sense of triple in a prevailing duple (usually compound duple) meter. See examples below.

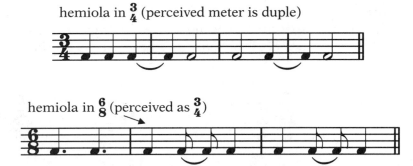

Stems, Beams and Flags, Ties, Vertical Alignment

Conventions for stem placement are as follows: In single-line music, notes in the lower half of the staff have stems up. Up stems belong on the right side of the noteheads. A note on the middle staff line may have an up or a down stem. Above the middle staff line, notes have stems down. Down stems belong on the left side of the noteheads. Up and down stems are also frequently used to identify two different parts on a single line.

In traditional notation, *flags on single (unbeamed) notes are drawn to the right only. Beams should connect small note values within the beat,* and across weak beats, but not across strong beats.

Ties are used to extend notes across bar lines and across strong beats. A tie is often the notational means of showing the location of a strong beat. Tie noteheads together, not stems. In chords, each note that is extended needs its own tie.

Rhythmic notation is rarely exact in terms of spacing proportion within each measure, but it usually gives more space to long events than to short ones. Take care to *align all simultaneous events vertically.* Intelligibility in notation depends on the eye detecting in general which events are longer and shorter, and which are simultaneous.

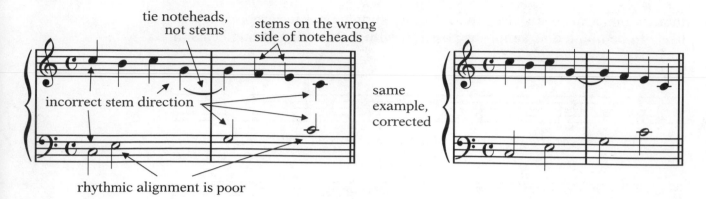

tie noteheads, not stems

stems on the wrong side of noteheads

incorrect stem direction

same example, corrected

rhythmic alignment is poor

TRIADS

A **triad** is a three-note chord built in thirds from its lowest note. One may also think of a triad as a third and a fifth built above a starting note. The members of the triad from bottom to top are the **root,** the **third,** and the **fifth.** Although the triad can be rearranged (revoiced) or inverted (arranged so that the root is not on the bottom), it can always be put into its most basic configuration: root, third, fifth. If the root is on the bottom, the triad is said to be in **root position** (it need not have the third and fifth directly above the root to be in root position, as long as the root is on the bottom).

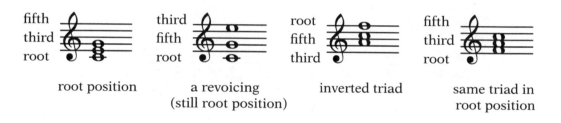

fifth
third
root

root position

third
fifth
root

a revoicing
(still root position)

root
fifth
third

inverted triad

fifth
third
root

same triad in
root position

Chord Quality

A triad consists of two stacked thirds. Since each of these thirds may be major or minor, there are four possible types of triads: if the bottom third is major and the top is minor (C-E, E-G, for example), the triad (C-E-G) is called *major.* If the bottom third is minor and the top is major (C-E♭-G, for example), the triad is called *minor.* If both thirds are minor (as in C-E♭-G♭), the triad is *diminished.* If both thirds are major (C-E-G♯, for example), the triad is *augmented.* The designation of triads as major, minor, diminished, or augmented is called **chord quality.**

Constructing Triads from Scales

Triads belonging to a given key are constructed from the scale of that key. Each triad is named for the scale step that is its root. The triads can also be named with *Roman numerals,* with I signifying the tonic, or triad built on the first scale step, V signifying the dominant, or triad built on the fifth scale step, etc.

Many musicians use a system of Roman numeral labeling that indicates chord quality as well as root-scale degree for each triad. In this system, uppercase Roman numerals are used for major triads; lowercase

Roman numerals for minor triads; a small circle superscript for diminished, and a small plus sign superscript for augmented. See the triads derived from C major below.

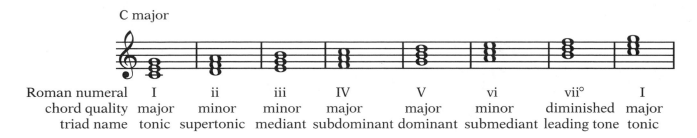

Roman numeral	I	ii	iii	IV	V	vi	vii°	I
chord quality	major	minor	minor	major	major	minor	diminished	major
triad name	tonic	supertonic	mediant	subdominant	dominant	submediant	leading tone	tonic

Compare the triads derived from c minor, below. Note that all the minor-scale triads, except for the mediant, are derived from the harmonic minor scale.

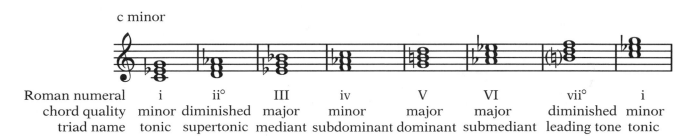

Roman numeral	i	ii°	III	iv	V	VI	vii°	i
chord quality	minor	diminished	major	minor	major	major	diminished	minor
triad name	tonic	supertonic	mediant	subdominant	dominant	submediant	leading tone	tonic

The basic triads for minor keys (except the mediant chord) are derived from the harmonic minor scale. Since the seventh scale step is raised in the harmonic minor, the dominant triad is major, and the leading tone triad is diminished, just as in major keys.

The triad built on the third scale step in minor (mediant or III chord) uses as its fifth the *lowered* seventh scale step; thus the triad is major, not augmented as it would be using a raised seventh scale step. While one sometimes sees the augmented III⁺ chord in musical literature, it is usually an unstable version of V rather than an independent triad.

While minor key triads are generally derived from the harmonic minor scale, the melodic minor also has the potential to generate triads. Some of these chords occur quite frequently, brought about by the use of the melodic minor in melody, bass line, or counterpoint. Particularly common in a minor key context are the major IV and minor v. The triad built on the lowered seventh scale step (VII) is frequently seen, especially associated harmonically with the triad III.

Relationships among the various triads, and the topic of chord function and harmonic progression are discussed in Part 3 of this book.

PART 2

Species Counterpoint

Counterpoint is music in which two or more melodic lines sound simultaneously. Contrapuntal textures occur in many musical styles, from medieval music to jazz. In this book, two types of counterpoint are introduced: first, in this section, species counterpoint, and tonal counterpoint in Part 4.

Species counterpoint is a system for gaining contrapuntal technique that was developed out of the style of Palestrina and other sixteenth-century composers. As a tool for learning counterpoint, it supplies a very controlled and gradual introduction to melodic formation and the treatment of dissonance. It should be understood, however, that there is no musical literature in species counterpoint—it is for study only.

Systematic training in counterpoint has been a traditional part of musical study for at least 250 years. Bach, Handel, Haydn, Mozart, Beethoven, Schubert, and Brahms (to name only a few) studied species counterpoint, and the principles of melodic coherence contained in the species form a foundation for the structure of all tonal music. Since species counterpoint is a technical study as opposed to a stylistic one, its specific rules vary somewhat from author to author and from teacher to teacher, according to the specific goals of the course and the level of the students. The technique is introduced here for the purpose of providing experience with melodic line as a whole, with intervals, with principles of consonance and dissonance, and with the concepts of beginning, middle, and end. The more historical aspects of sixteenth-century counterpoint, particularly the use of the church modes, lie outside the scope of this presentation. Students seeking a more thorough course in species counterpoint will find some helpful references listed at the end of Part 2.

The study of species consists of exercises in writing counterpoint against a given line, called the *cantus firmus* (or CF). Each of the species has a particular rhythmic identity in relation to the cantus, and particular issues of dissonance treatment. The five species are note against note, two notes against one, four against one, offbeat two against one (suspensions), and florid, which is a combination of the other four. To practice species counterpoint, exercises should be written both above and below a cantus firmus.

The following outline of species counterpoint contains a large number of rules, which may seem overly restrictive to students eager to express themselves musically. Remember that the purpose of the rules is not to stifle creativity, but to *focus* it. The goal in species counterpoint is to create melodies that are beautiful, flowing, and coherent.

FIRST SPECIES

In **first species,** a melodic line in whole notes is written against a given line (cantus firmus—CF) in whole notes. Note that all examples in this book are in major and minor keys, as opposed to church modes.

Melodic Line

The following rules and guidelines serve the purpose of keeping the melodic line flowing and unbroken. The "forbidden" intervals are those that tend to break up the line. These rules apply to the melodic line itself (upper or lower part). The counterpoint, that is, the relationship of the line to the CF, is discussed below.

Intervals in a Melodic Line

Permitted: all major and minor intervals up to and including the major 6th; octaves.

Forbidden: all augmented and diminished intervals; all sevenths; all skips greater than an octave. No chromaticism is allowed. The only accidentals that may appear are those that raise or lower the sixth and seventh scale degrees in minor keys.

Skips in the Melodic Line

Two consecutive skips in the same direction should not equal more than an octave and should not outline a seventh. These rules also apply to situations in which there are more than two consecutive skips in the same direction.

Skips imply a change of direction to follow. The leap of an octave must be preceded and followed by a change of direction (see 1 & 2 below). The large interval or pair of skips totalling a large interval is an unusual event. The large skip is followed by a filling-in with smaller intervals, mostly steps (see 3 & 4 below).

When skips are not filled in, one hears the line divided into several voices because of the separation of registers.

This line seems to have two voices, an upper voice answered by a lower voice. This effect should be avoided. Large skips should be filled in so that all registers sound connected, like a single voice.

Melodic Line: Beginning, Middle, and End

A coherent line has a clear sense of beginning, middle, and end. The following rules and conventions are aimed at achieving this coherence.

Beginning

The upper part should begin on the first, third, or fifth scale degree; the lower part begins on the tonic note.

Middle

The middle should show direction, moving from the first note toward a **climax** (high point), and from the climax toward the cadence. The high point should only appear once, and should never be the last note. It may, on rare occasion, be the first note. The high point *should not* be the leading tone, since this tone needs to resolve upward. Occasionally a low point may substitute.

Repeated patterns and sequences tend to divide the line into smaller units, destroying the sense of unbroken continuity from beginning to end. Repeated patterns and sequences should therefore be avoided (see below). Going over the same notes again and again should also be avoided, as this deprives the line of its direction and purpose (see the second example, below).

Repeated notes are occasionally possible. Use no more than one repeated note in each part.

avoid sequences, repeating patterns   don't go over and over the same notes

End

The end of a phrase, an exercise, or a whole piece is called the **cadence.**

The upper part may end on the tonic, or on the third or fifth scale step.

The lower part should cadence on the tonic note.

The approach to the last note should be as smooth as possible, promoting a sense of rest and completion. The following melodic cadence formulas help to achieve this goal. *Only these formulas* should be used for the last three notes of both upper and lower parts (they may be transposed to different scale degrees in the upper part). Observe that in all these patterns, all three notes are connected by step.

C major

Here are some examples of cadence patterns that might be acceptable in other contexts, but *should not* be used for the last three notes of an exercise in species counterpoint.

etc.

Counterpoint—Two Lines Together
Intervals

In first species, with both parts in whole notes, one note of the CF sounds against one note of the counterpoint. The interval between the upper voice and the lower voice must be consonant at all times.

Consonant Intervals

Unison, octave, major and minor 3rds and 6ths, perfect 5ths, and any of these plus an octave.

Dissonant Intervals

All augmented and diminished intervals, major and minor 2nds and 7ths, perfect 4ths.

Independence of Voices: Parallel Motion, Octaves, and Fifths

The independence of the parts is a prime objective of counterpoint. There-fore *parallel octaves and fifths are forbidden. Direct octaves and fifths are also forbidden.* A direct octave or fifth is an octave or fifth that is ap-proached from the same direction by both the upper and lower voice. Octaves and fifths must be approached in contrary motion. Parallel unisons are forbidden.

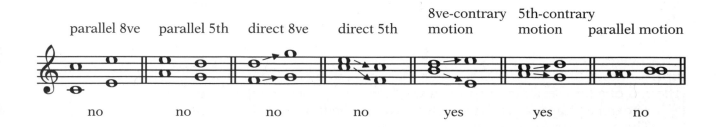

Parallel thirds and sixths are fine, but too many of them in succession destroy the independence of the parts. This is even more of a problem when a change of direction is involved (see 1 below). The independence of the voices is also weakened if both parts skip in the same direction at the same time (see 2 on the following page).

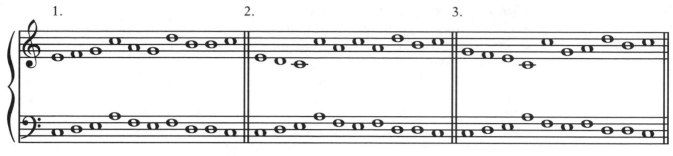

C major

      1. voices not independent

      2. Better, but big skip in same direction at the same time in both voices is weak.

      3. This is better, voices are more independent.

General Observations

The greatest independence of the voices is attained when they move in contrary motion, but contrary motion at all times is not necessary, possible, or even desirable. For greater independence, avoid making the high point at the same moment in both voices. Voice crossings are allowed. Remember that the general object is to write two smooth, coherent, and independent parts.

It is extremely important to connect contrapuntal rules to actual sounds: *Play or sing all examples and exercises!*

SECOND SPECIES

In **second species**, a melodic line in **half notes** is written against the whole notes of the CF.

Melodic Line

First species rules (intervals, skips, etc.) apply to second species melodies also.

Counterpoint

Rhythm

Each whole note of the CF constitutes one measure. Each measure is divided into a strong beat (first half note) and a weak beat (second half note). The counterpoint may begin with a half rest, but no other rests are allowed. In second species there should be no repeated notes. The last measure will be a whole note, and the next-to-last measure may be either a whole note or two half notes.

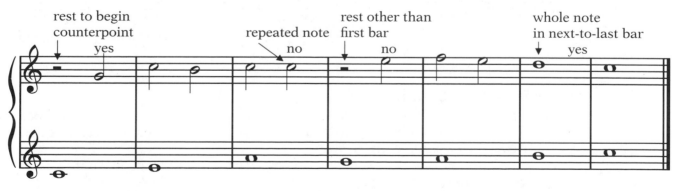

rest to begin counterpoint — yes

repeated note — no

rest other than first bar — no

whole note in next-to-last bar — yes

C major

Consonance and Dissonance

On the *strong beat*, the interval between the CF and the counterpoint *must be consonant* (therefore octave, unison, m3, M3, P5, m6, M6, or any of these plus an octave).

On the *weak beat*, the interval between the CF and the counterpoint *may be dissonant* if the dissonance is treated as a *passing tone*. A **passing tone** is a dissonant note that is approached by step and left by step in the same direction. The passing tone (P.T.) serves to connect two consonant notes of the counterpoint that are a third apart.

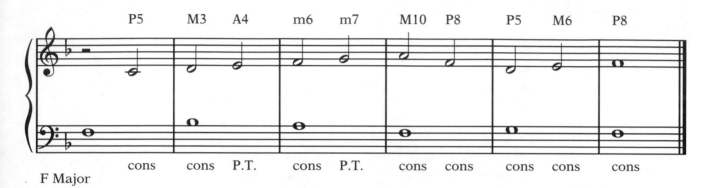

Note that a weak beat may be a consonance, in which case no special rules apply to it; all skips in second species involve consonances. If the weak beat is a dissonance, it must be a passing tone. Remember that a *P.T. must pass by step between two consonances*, and must continue the line in the same direction (see example below).

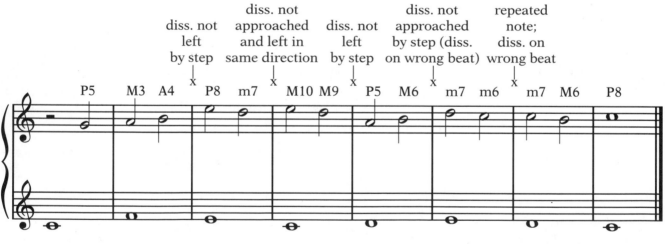

Fifths and Octaves

Parallel fifths and octaves are forbidden between *consecutive beats* (in other words, from weak beat to strong beat); octaves and fifths are also forbidden between *consecutive strong beats*.

Fifths or octaves occurring on consecutive weak beats are not considered parallel.

Direct fifths and octaves are forbidden between consecutive beats.

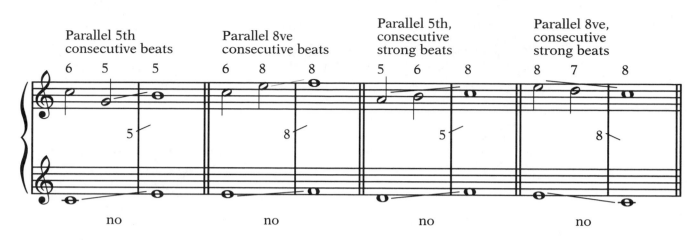

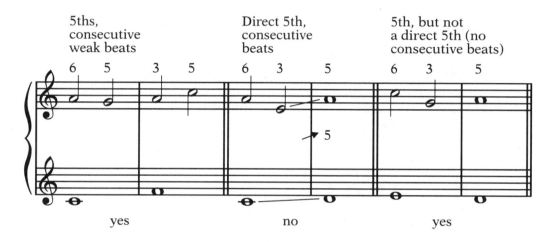

Beginning, Middle, and End

The rules and conventions remain the same in second species as in first. Remember that the lower part must begin and end on the tonic.

The high point may be on either a weak or a strong beat.

The cadence pattern (in terms of pitch, not rhythm) should be one of those given for first species.

THIRD SPECIES

In **third species**, four quarter notes are written against each whole note of the CF. There should be no repeated notes. In this metric context, the first beat of the measure is the strongest, and the third beat is also relatively strong. Beats 2 and 4 are metrically weak.

Consonance and Dissonance

Within the melodic line, and between the two voices, classification of consonant and dissonant intervals is the same as has already been defined for first and second species.

Every downbeat must be consonant. *Beats 2, 3, and 4 may be consonant or dissonant.* Three types of dissonance are permitted in third species.

These are:

1. *Passing tone*—The **passing tone** is a stepwise connection between two consonances that are a third apart. The passing tone must be approached and left in the same direction, up or down. Passing tones may be unaccented (beats 2 and 4) or accented (beat 3). Do not use a dissonant passing tone on beat 1.

2. *Neighbor tone*—The **neighbor tone** is a step above or below a consonant note. In the music of the sixteenth century, from which the species are derived, the lower neighbor is much more commonly used than the upper neighbor. The neighbor tone is approached by step from a consonant note, and returns to that same note. Neighbor tones may occur on beats 2 or 4.

3. *Cambiata*—The **cambiata** is a five-note figure starting on a downbeat. The succession of intervals within the five-note figure is fixed: From the consonant downbeat, the line moves down by step, down by third, up by step, up by step into next downbeat (see example below). The first, third, and fourth beats, and the downbeat of the next measure, are all consonant. *The second beat is dissonant, and is left by skip.* The example shows how the second and third beats embellish a falling third between the first beat and the fourth beat.

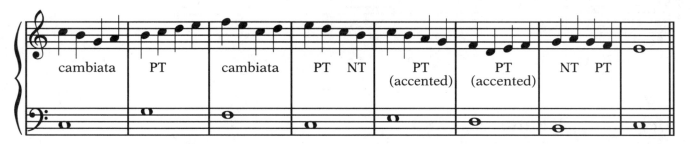

C major

Note the unusual features of the cambiata figure:

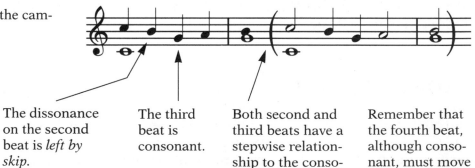

The dissonance on the second beat is *left by skip*.

The third beat is consonant.

Both second and third beats have a stepwise relationship to the consonant fourth beat.

Remember that the fourth beat, although consonant, must move by step up to the next downbeat.

It should be noted that different teachers may wish to put more or fewer restrictions on the use of the cambiata figure, since both its application in various periods and its definition by various theorists have been somewhat changeable.

Fifths and Octaves
Parallel fifths and octaves are to be avoided between these beats:

    beat 1 and beat 1 of the next measure

    beat 3 and beat 1 of the next measure

    beat 4 and beat 1 of the next measure

Direct fifths and octaves are to be avoided between beat 4 and beat 1 of the next measure. Direct fifths and octaves between beats 1, 2, or 3 and the next downbeat may also be objectionable. These cases must be considered individually.

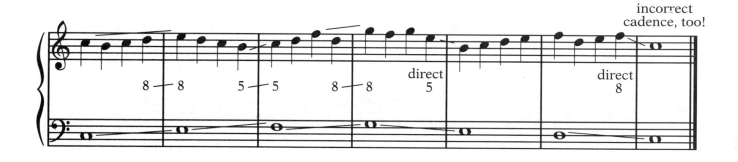

Beginning, Middle, and End
Lower parts must begin and end on the tonic. Upper parts may begin on any note in the tonic triad. Any beat is acceptable for the first note of the counterpoint.

    Rules about the *high point* are unchanged from first and second species. The high point should occur on a strong beat. With the great quantity of notes available in third species, it is particularly important to organize the line around the high point and the cadence. This can be done, for example, by establishing preliminary high points as the line gradually ascends to its climax, or by moving to temporary goals on the way to the cadence.

    The primary form of motion should be stepwise, but skips can be used to good advantage in pointing the direction of the line. Skips of a fourth or more should generally be introduced and left with a change of direction, and large skips should be filled in as the line continues. Avoid long cascades of notes in one direction or the other, and use arpeggiated triads very sparingly.

Approaching the Cadence
The last measure is a whole note in both parts. The next-to-last measure in the counterpoint may be either four quarters or two quarters followed by a half note. The approach to the cadence should be by step. In the next-to-last measure, the dissonance treatment may be relaxed to allow a *double neighbor* figure as an ornamentation of a clear cadence. The dissonant second and third beats of double neighbor figure are also often called **changing tones.**

E and G are neighbors to F

C and A are neighbors to B

Here is an example of third species. Analyze the intervals as consonant, or as specific dissonances. Note the gradual ascent to the high point, the gradual descent to the cadence, and the prevailing stepwise motion.

G major

FOURTH SPECIES

In **fourth species**, *syncopated half notes* are written against the CF. There should be no repeated notes. The first half note of the measure is the "strong" half, the second is the "weak" half.

Consonance and Dissonance

Within the melodic line and between the two parts, definitions of consonance and dissonance are the same as for first, second, and third species.

Every weak half must be consonant. The *strong half*, which is tied over from the previous measure, *may be either consonant or dissonant*. If it is dissonant, the strong half must be treated as a **suspension.** A suspension dissonance is handled in three steps:

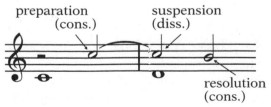

preparation (cons.)

suspension (diss.)

resolution (cons.)

1. the **preparation** is a consonance occurring on a weak beat, which is
2. tied over (a *suspension*) to the following strong beat. The CF moves during the tied note, creating a dissonance on the strong beat;
3. the **resolution** occurs as the dissonance steps down to a consonance on the next weak beat.

Upper Part Counterpoint

When the upper part is the counterpoint, the possible suspensions are:

1. the interval of a seventh resolving to a sixth (7–6)
2. the interval of a fourth resolving to a third (4–3)
3. more rarely, the interval of a ninth resolving to an octave (9–8, see example below)

F major

The *augmented 4th*, whose upper voice may possess a strong tendency to resolve upward, presents a special problem in a 4–3 suspension. It may be used only in the midst of an already established stepwise descending line in the counterpoint.

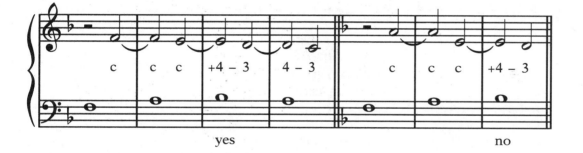

The *9–8 suspension* is occasionally possible for the upper part counterpoint. However, the effect of the strong dissonance resolving to the most static of consonances will disrupt the flow and tension between the two lines unless it is handled with care. Use the 9–8 suspension (upper part only) *only if both voices approach it by step, in contrary motion.*

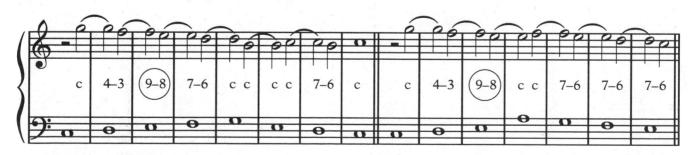

9–8 suspension: both voices approach by step in contrary motion

It isn't necessary to continue the stepwise contrary motion after the 9–8 suspension is resolved to the octave.

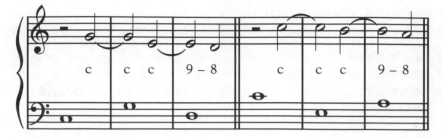

These are examples of incorrect 9–8 suspensions, They are wrong because the approach is wrong, and the octave is overemphasized.

Lower Part Counterpoint

The only permissible dissonant suspension in the lower part is the 2–3 suspension. The lower part relies heavily on consonant syncopations.

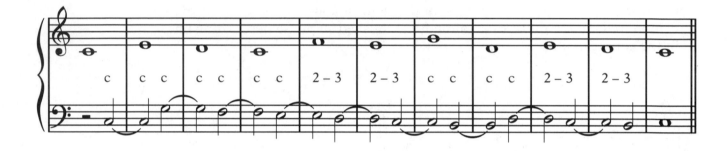

Octaves and Fifths

In fourth species, *the weak beats are emphasized,* because they receive the accent of resolution. *Octaves and fifths on consecutive weak beats sound parallel and are therefore forbidden.* It may help to think of the syncopated counterpoint as a first species line lagging behind the CF. See examples of parallel fifths and octaves below. Since the strong beats are heard as relatively unstable in fourth species, it is possible to write fifths or octaves on consecutive strong beats.

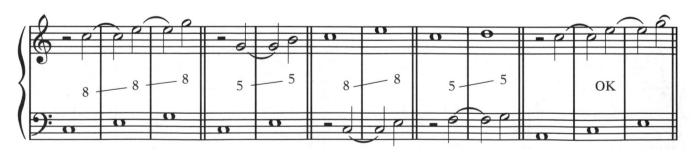

parallel 5ths and 8ves

strong beat 8ves—
correct (but not ideal
as counterpoint)

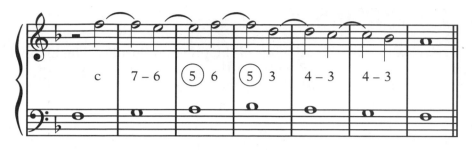

Fifths on consecutive strong beats are perfectly acceptable in fourth species. There is another set of strong beat fifths in the example in the middle of page 28.

Beginning, Middle, and End

The counterpoint may begin on either beat. The upper part must begin and end on a note in the tonic triad; the lower part must begin and end on the tonic note. Make sure to include a high point. The last note is a whole note, not tied over. Approach the cadence by step, using a dissonant suspension coming into the next-to-last bar, if possible.

For example:

Once in an exercise, you may break out of the suspension pattern. In this situation, the rules of second species apply. The purpose of this break is to improve the line, often by breaking up a long stepwise chain of suspensions.

FIFTH SPECIES

Fifth species is a combination of all the previous species. The characteristic rhythms of second, third, and fourth species are freely mixed to form a flowing counterpoint to the whole notes of the CF.

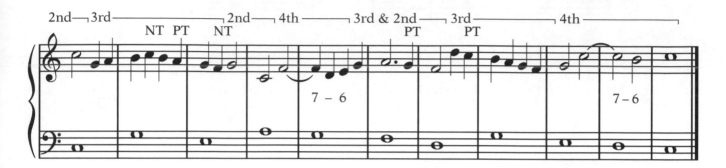

The example shows the way in which each note of the counterpoint can be understood as belonging to a particular species. Each group of notes must follow the rules for the species to which it belongs. This is especially important for the treatment of dissonance. Therefore, you should adhere to the rules of each species exactly as you have already learned them, except for the following changes and comments.

First species: The exercise will always end with a whole note in each part. Whole notes elsewhere in the counterpoint disrupt the flow of the line, and should be avoided.

Second species: There are no changes in the rules for second species; the strong half note must be a consonance, and the weak half may be consonant also. If the weak half is dissonant, it must be a passing tone. The dotted half note is a combination of second and third species ($\downarrow \downarrow = \downarrow \downarrow \downarrow$). Fifth species tends to be heard in half note beats, with the second and fourth quarters in each measure heard as weak beats or upbeats. The rhythm $\downarrow \downarrow$ supports this metric arrangement. On the other hand, the rhythms $\downarrow \downarrow$ and $\downarrow \downarrow \downarrow$ undermine the strength of the half note by stressing the weak second beat. These syncopations are not allowed in fifth species.

Third species: Third species rules are unchanged. Remember that passing tones must pass to consonances by step, and that a neighbor tone steps away from a consonance and steps back to that same consonance. Cambiata and double neighbor figures may be used in fifth species.

Fourth species: The rules for fourth species are basically unchanged. In order to avoid weak quarter syncopation, the fourth beat cannot be tied over the bar line. *Remember that in fourth species, the weak half must be consonant.* The available dissonant suspensions are the same as you have already learned, 7–6, 4–3, and sometimes 9–8 in the upper part; use only 2–3 suspensions (and consonant syncopations) if the lower voice is the counterpoint. *Suspensions in fifth species always resolve on the third beat* (the second half note of the measure), as you have learned. However, this resolution may be embellished by a quarter note on the second beat. This embellishing quarter note should either be a consonance or a neighbor to the note of resolution.

For example, this fourth species line could become:

Beginning, Middle, and End

The counterpoint may begin on any beat. As usual, the lower part must begin on the tonic, and the upper part must begin on a note in the tonic triad.

Compose your line around an ascent to the high point, and a descent to the cadence. To maintain the rhythmic flow, do not start a series of quarter notes on the downbeat. The one exception is two quarters followed by a tied half note. Suspensions help to keep the rhythm flowing. Avoid sequences, including purely rhythmic ones.

If possible, use a suspension on the downbeat of the bar preceding the cadence. A cadence introduced in this way is often called a **suspension cadence.** In a suspension cadence, the resolution may be embellished with eighth notes (see example below). The addition of eighth notes to the texture creates a special quality of rhythmic saturation, the tension of which is released in the cadential bar. Eighth notes may be used only in the next-to-last measure.

SUGGESTIONS FOR ANALYSIS AND FURTHER READING

Analysis

Since species counterpoint was developed initially as a technique builder for counterpoint in the style of Palestrina, it is helpful to look at music in this style when studying species. Especially useful for two-part writing are the *Cantiones Duarum Vocum* (two-voice motets) by Roland de Lassus. Masses and motets of Palestrina and of other sixteenth-century composers, such as William Byrd and Tomás Luis de Victoria, are also excellent works for study.

Further reading

Students who wish to consult the original source for species counterpoint should look for Johann Joseph Fux, *Gradus ad Parnassum*, translated from the Latin by Alfred Mann (W. W. Norton). The more modern classic text on this subject is Knud Jeppesen's *Counterpoint*, translated by Glen Haydon (Prentice-Hall). A good recent text on sixteenth-century counterpoint (though not specifically species) is *The Craft of Modal Counterpoint* by Thomas Benjamin (Schirmer Books–Macmillan).

PART 3

Harmony and Voice Leading

This outline of harmony summarizes the general mechanics of chord formation, progression, and voice leading in the **common practice period** (roughly 1700–1900). It is not intended as a guide for composing, but rather as an aid in gaining technique in a familiar style. The "rules" cited here are not necessarily laws which the composers of the Baroque, Classical, and Romantic periods consciously followed, but rather a generalized summary of their harmonic practice, as gathered from the enormous body of their works.

Formal studies undertaken by composers from these periods usually emphasized counterpoint. Harmonic progression was likely to be viewed as the working out of interwoven voices over the beginning, middle, and end of a phrase, not as a succession of isolated verticalities. Although this outline allows for a chord-to-chord approach, it is very desirable to think in terms of melodic continuity of individual voices, particularly the outer voices, within each phrase you write or analyze. It is also important to develop your recognition of larger groups and patterns of chords within the span of a phrase. This aspect of technique can be greatly enhanced by practicing cadential progressions and other common fragments as exercises in keyboard harmony. Many common patterns are given for practice at the back of the book.

In four-part harmony, four separate voices moving together make up chords. The four voices are **soprano** (stem up in treble clef), **alto** (stem down in treble clef), **tenor** (stem up in bass clef), and **bass** (stem down in bass clef).

We can begin by setting up a four-voice chord in root position: The root is in the bass, and another root (this is called **doubling**) is in one of the upper voices. The notes may be spaced closely together (if they are as close as possible, they are said to be in **close position**) or they may be more spread out (**open position**). There should not be more than an octave between soprano and alto, or between alto and tenor. There may be more than an

close
position   open
position

octave between tenor and bass. In general, triadic harmony seems to be more sonorous if there is less space between the three upper voices, and more between tenor and bass.

The movement of each voice from one chord to the next is called **voice leading.** There are may subtleties in the study of voice leading, but a guiding principle is this: Four-part writing should preserve the independence of the four voices.

Lines moving in *parallel octaves, parallel fifths, and parallel unisons* tend to be perceived as doublings rather than independent voices. For this reason, *parallel octaves, fifths, and unisons are not allowed between any two voices as one chord moves to the next.* Parallel thirds, fourths, and sixths are fine, but too much parallelism at any interval will eventually weaken the sense of a full four-part texture.

Direct octaves and fifths are octaves or fifths approached by two voices from the same direction. While these are usually avoided in two-part textures, *they are perfectly acceptable in four-part writing if the upper voice moves to the octave or fifth by step, while the lower voice moves by skip.*

To maintain the integrity of each of the four parts, *augmented and diminished intervals are avoided melodically,* though they may occasionally be used in the bass voice. In general, conjunct (i.e., stepwise) motion and small skips are normal for the three upper parts; the bass line is more likely to have larger skips than are the upper voices, but the bass also often moves by step. The soprano voice is more prominent melodically than either the alto or the tenor. At the beginning of the study of harmony, there is very little melodic flexibility in the soprano or any other part. As technique in harmony increases, added flexibility in voice leading will allow for the construction of a good soprano line (or harmonization of an existing tune) to become the major goal.

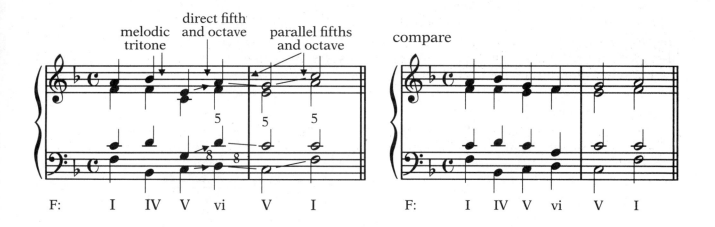

ROOT POSITION, COMMON TONE VOICE LEADING

To move from chord to chord in root position, follow the rules of **common tone voice leading:**

1. Double the root (except as noted below).
2. Keep all common tones (CT) in the voices in which they originate; move other voices to the closest note in the new chord. Between two chords, there will be one common tone if root movement is by fourth or fifth; two if root movement is by third (or sixth).
3. There are no common tones if root movement is by step. In this case all three upper voices move in contrary motion to the bass, each upper voice moving to the closest note in the new chord.

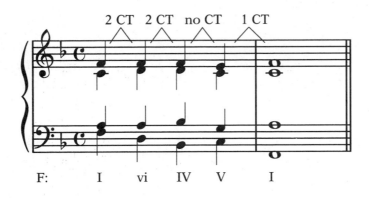

F: I   vi   IV   V   I

Three Exceptions to Common Tone Rules in Root Position:

1. *Deceptive cadence (V–vi).* There are no common tones between V and vi, therefore we expect all three upper voices to move *down* in contrary motion to the bass. An exception occurs when the leading tone in V follows its melodic tendency to resolve *up* to the tonic note in the vi chord. The resulting vi chord has a doubled third instead of the usual doubled root. Note that the progression works the same way in minor mode. V–vi is not always treated as a deceptive cadence. See example 1 below.

2. *VI–V in minor keys.* The normal voice leading and doublings produce an *augmented second* from the doubled root of VI to the leading tone of V (see example 2 below). This problem is solved by doubling the third of VI instead of the root. One of the doubled thirds steps down to the leading tone; the other two upper voices step up as usual.

3. *ii–V.* Although there is one common tone in this progression, it is frequently treated as though there were none; in this case the three upper voices all descend to the closest note in the V chord. In major keys you may use either the common tone voice leading, or the all-descending pattern. In minor mode, the diminished ii chord rarely appears in root position. If it does, you must bring all three upper voices down when moving to V. This procedure avoids the *augmented second* that occurs if the common tone is kept (see example 3 below).

1.

Deceptive cadence

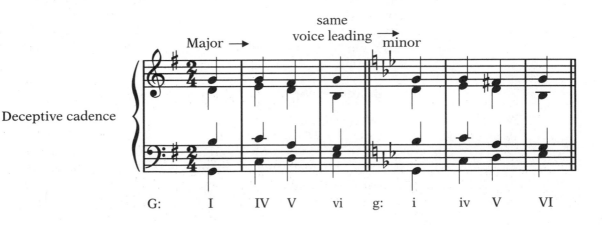

G: I   IV   V   vi   g: i   iv   V   VI

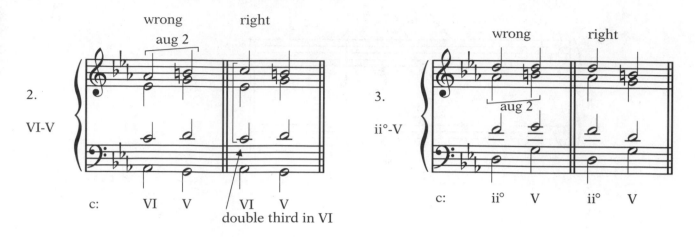

HARMONIC PROGRESSION

The language of tonal music depends on the idea of **harmonic progression.** Progression means directed motion, or movement toward a goal, and harmonic progression therefore implies harmonic movement that is goal-directed. While any series of chords may be played in succession with more or less pleasing results, a *progression* of chords is moving toward a goal, and each harmony in the progression can be understood in terms of its place in that motion.

In order to understand the notion of harmonic progression, we must return to the idea that phrases have a beginning, middle, and end. This was discussed in species counterpoint in terms of melodic considerations: Certain pitches were appropriate for beginning a line, certain cadence patterns were possible for ending, and the nature of the middle had to do with building to a high point and then connecting smoothly to the cadence. In building coherent harmonic progressions, two new considerations must be added: One concerns the specific functions of individual harmonies within a key; the other expands the definition of cadence.

Function in harmony can be divided into three main types: **tonic function** provides central context and identity for beginning, as well as rest and repose, the ultimate end goal of harmonic motion. **Dominant function** means a lack of repose; the dominant specifically seeks the tonic for resolution. **Subdominant or pre-dominant function** is less dynamic than dominant; it seeks the tonic also, but more often than not moves to the dominant before arriving on the tonic.

The main harmonic functions can be summarized as I, IV, and V. These are sometimes called the **primary chords** in a key. The other harmonies fit in as follows:

ii—in major and minor, generally plays a pre-dominant role.

iii—in major, having two notes in common with both tonic and dominant triads, lacks a strong function; sometimes used in circle of fifths progressions to go to vi; in minor, III is the tonic of the relative major. It functions as an alternative to the minor tonic and is an important pole of harmonic activity.

vi—in major and minor, belongs ultimately to the pre-dominant group, but can substitute (temporarily) for I in a cadence formula, creating a deceptive cadence.

vii°—a weaker version of the dominant function, vii° seeks resolution to I.

Note that the pre-dominant chords ii and IV tend to move on to V, but V goes to I, not to ii or IV.

With the idea of harmonic function in mind, it is possible to appreciate coherence in chord progressions:

I – IV – V – I.   Same idea expanded: I – IV – V – vi – IV – ii – V – I.

tonic   subdominant   dominant   tonic

tonic   subdominant   dominant   deceptive cadence   pre-dominant   dominant   tonic

CADENCES

Harmonic progressions are goal-oriented, and the goal of the progression is the cadence—the end. In species counterpoint only a few cadence formulas were allowed, but in harmony, many different cadence types are possible. In terms of chord progression, we can consider four basic cadence types:

Full or authentic cadence: V – I (called **perfect authentic cadence** if the tonic note is in the soprano of the I chord; called **imperfect authentic cadence** if $\hat{3}$ or $\hat{5}$ is in the soprano of the I chord). Perfect authentic is the most final of cadences.

Half cadence: a cadence on V. Not heard as final, a half cadence creates the need for an answering full cadence.

Deceptive cadence: V – vi. Not a final cadence, prolongs the tension in a progression toward a full cadence.

Plagal cadence: IV – I. Can be a final cadence, coming after a V–I full cadence (the "amen" ending).

There is a more detailed description of cadence types at the beginning of Part 5, page 87.

What makes a succession of chords a cadence? We wouldn't call every V–I succession a cadence, and some full cadences sound much more final than others. Factors that influence our perception of cadence include *melody* (the top voice): Does it sound complete? Does it end on the tonic, as opposed to the third or fifth?; *the bass line:* Does its line sound complete? Is the cadence in root position?; *rhythm:* Is the cadence on a weak or strong beat?; *phrase context:* Does this cadence resemble others in the same piece? Does the phrase length balance others in context? Does the phrase have a clear beginning, middle, and end? As knowledge of harmony increases, sensitivity to these other factors must also increase. Through listening and analysis it will become clear that the different combinations of phrase shapes and cadences make pieces unique, while the underlying logic of function and cadence type makes pieces coherent.

SOME NOTES ON DOUBLING

Almost all tonal music uses root position triads with root doublings, *at times*. But the musical literature shows clearly that chords are often not in root position, and that doublings other than root doubling are common. The study of inversions (chords not in root position) is taken up at length below. The new material contains many rules and suggestions for doublings.

Alternative doublings introduce a new flexibility into voice leading. In general, whether in root position or inversion, doubling decisions (other than always-double-the-root) tend to reinforce the **tonal degrees** of the scale. The tonal degrees are $\hat{1}$, $\hat{2}$, $\hat{4}$, and $\hat{5}$. These, especially $\hat{1}$, $\hat{4}$, and $\hat{5}$, are roots of the most key-defining harmonies, and are also the scale steps that are the same in both major and minor modes of a given key. Doubling the tonal degrees means that, as an alternative to root doubling, one would tend to double the fifth of the I chord (as opposed to the third), the third of the ii chord (as opposed to the fifth), and so on. Less commonly, the so-called **modal degrees,** $\hat{3}$ and $\hat{6}$, may be doubled, especially if doing so creates a good soprano line. The **leading tone** should never be doubled in V or vii.

On the next pages are discussions of inverted chords, seventh chords, and various kinds of chromaticism. These all play important roles in shaping the beginnings, middles, and ends of phrases. The new materials are presented in relation to the primary (I, IV, V) functions, and often in the context of cadential formulas. It is especially important to play the examples, and to learn to hear each new pattern so that you will recognize it in actual pieces.

CHORDS IN INVERSION

An inverted triad is one in which the third or fifth is in the bass voice, rather than the root. If the third is in the bass, this is called **first inversion;** if the fifth is in the bass, this is called **second inversion.**

Triads in first inversion are used to vary the sonority of chords, to give melodic direction and flexibility to the bass line, and to lighten the functional weight of some triads. There are very few rules to govern the use of first inversion chords, since their substitution for root position and their doublings are often matters of taste or convenience in a particular context. Some suggestions are given later.

Second inversion chords are used much less freely than first inversion. In second inversion, the perfect 4th between the bass note (fifth of the chord) and the root is considered a dissonance, and requires special treatment. Therefore, *chords in second inversion can't simply substitute for root position or first inversion* as a means of providing variety. The proper use of second inversion chords is taken up as a separate topic below.

Compare the first inversion triad to root position. In root position, the intervals above the bass note are octave, third (tenth), and fifth. In first inversion, the intervals present are sixth and third (the bass could also be doubled at the octave). The interval of the sixth is characteristic of first inversion, and for this reason, Roman numerals indicating first inversion include a "6" in superscript: I^6, ii^6, etc.

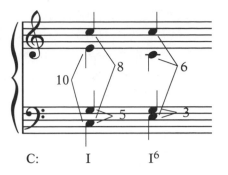

Looking at a second inversion triad, one sees intervals of octave, fourth, and sixth above the bass. Both the fourth and the sixth are characteristic of second inversion as opposed to root position. The Roman numeral shorthand for second inversion is $^6_4$, I^6_4, IV^6_4, etc.

FIRST INVERSION

Inverted chords add melodic flexibility to the bass line and allow the primary functions (I, IV, and V) to be weakened while still remaining recognizable. There is no definite rule that can be applied to the use and doubling of every first inversion chord. The greater complexity requires more awareness of possible pitfalls (fifths, octaves, augmented and diminished intervals) as well as greater sensitivity in the creation of individual lines, particularly the soprano line.

Some General Observations

I^6 is more likely to double the root or fifth, less likely to double the third (bass), especially in major mode, unless there is good melodic reason. I^6 is a lighter version of tonic function and has many uses, but is not a final cadential goal. For full cadences, use root position.

ii^6 generally doubles the third (bass) when going to V. In this very common pattern, all three upper voices descend to the closest note in the V chord—don't keep the common tone. In other contexts (not moving to V), ii^6 may double the root or third.

iii^6 is an unstable chord in major because of its similarity to V; doubling should promote general smoothness. In minor, III^6 is a more strongly functional chord and any doubling is possible.

IV^6 in major tends to pass between V and V^6. All doublings are possible. In minor, fifth or root doubling is usual. A common progression in minor is iv^6–V. Called a **phrygian cadence** because of its half step motion in the bass, this progression requires a doubled root or fifth in the iv^6 chord (a doubled third would move by an augmented second when iv^6 moved to V). The second example below ends with a phrygian cadence.

V⁶   doubles the root or fifth, chord moves to I. Don't double the third of V, as this is the leading tone.

vi⁶   unstable in major and minor because of its similarity to tonic triad; its doubling should promote smooth voice leading in its surrounding context.

vii°⁶ tends to pass between I and I⁶. Double the third or fifth, depending on the melodic context. Avoid doubling the leading tone.

A few examples:

USE AND DOUBLING OF ii⁶ CHORD (CADENTIAL)

ii⁶ is the functional equivalent of IV in cadential patterns, and is probably the most commonly used pre-dominant chord. It leads smoothly into full, deceptive, and half cadences:

ii⁶–V–I or (full cadence); ii⁶–V–VI (deceptive cadence); ii⁶–V (half cadence).

Cadential ii⁶ is very common in both major and minor contexts.

In cadential situations, *ii⁶ normally doubles the third* (the bass), which is the subdominant note of the scale. This doubling emphasizes the pre-dominant function of ii⁶.

In the progression ii⁶–V, the bass of ii⁶ steps up to the root of V. *All three upper voices of ii⁶ descend* to the closest note in the V chord. Compare the following progressions. Only one note changes when ii⁶ replaces IV. Play these in major and minor keys.

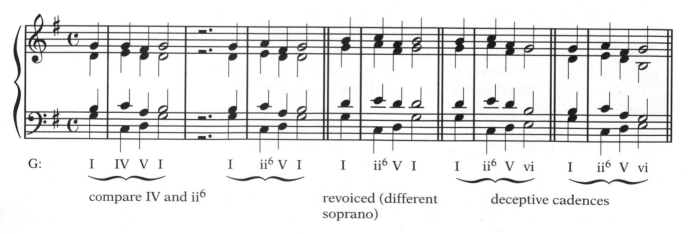

Note on voice leading: The ii⁶ chord often leads to the dominant, but it can move to other harmonies as well. The progression I–ii⁶ has the potential to create parallel fifths if the soprano of the tonic chord is the fifth. In the melodic succession $\hat{5}$–$\hat{6}$, IV would normally be used instead of ii⁶. For another potential voice leading problem involving ii⁶, see Second Inversion (cadential I$^6_4$), below.

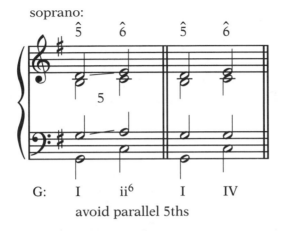

avoid parallel 5ths

NONHARMONIC TONES

Any note that is not a member of the triadic harmony on any given beat is a **nonharmonic tone.** Such a note is also called a **dissonance.** Most of the dissonances listed below have already been introduced in Part 2 of this book, but they can easily be learned by students who have not studied species counterpoint.

The several types of nonharmonic tones can be divided into two general catagories: those which usually occur on weak beats, and those which always occur on strong beats. In categorizing them further, it is necessary to see how each type relates melodically to the surrounding notes. The various weak beat and strong beat nonharmonic tones have specific patterns of approach and resolution which are defining characteristics and are, for the most part, strictly followed throughout the comon practice period. While most of the examples below show nonharmonic tones in the top voice, *they can occur in any voice of a musical texture, including the bass.*

Weak Beat Nonharmonic Tones

Name	Abbreviation	Approached by	Left by	Direction of Resolution	Example
passing tone	PT	step	step	same as approach	A
neighbor tone (upper or lower)	UN, LN	step	step	opposite of approach (back where it came from)	B
anticipation	ANT	step	repeats same tone	repeated note becomes chord tone	C

Strong Beat Nonharmonic Tones

Name	Abbreviation	Approached by	Left by	Direction of Resolution	Example
accented passing tone	APT	step	step	same as approach	D
suspension	SUS	same note tied or repeated	step	usually down	E
appoggiatura	AP	leap—or may begin a phrase	step	can step up or down	F

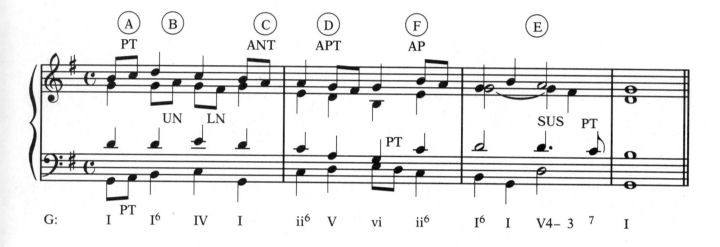

Combination Nonharmonic Tones

Name	Abbreviation	Description
échappée or escape tone	ECH	*An **échappée,** or **escape tone,** is a weak beat nonharmonic tone that may occur between two consonances that are a step apart. The échappée steps away from a consonance and skips by a third into its resolution. This is sometimes referred to as an incomplete neighbor tone.*

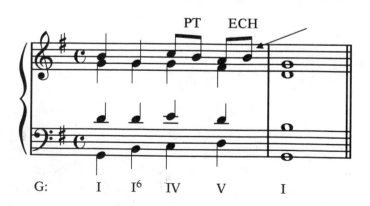

| cambiata | CAMB | A **cambiata** is a rhythmically weak figure connecting two consonances that are a third apart (see third species counterpoint). The classic cambiata steps down into a dissonance, then skips down by a third before stepping back into its resolution. The direction of the entire figure can also be reversed. Some theorists call any weak beat neighbor tone that is approached by skip and resolved by step a cambiata. |

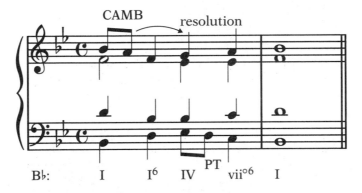

| double neighbor or changing tones | DN | A **double neighbor** is a combination of two neighbor tones, upper and lower, around the same pitch. This figure steps away from a chord tone, forming a neighbor, then leaps by a third to the other side of the starting tone before returning to it by step. This configuration is also called **changing tones.** Because the first dissonant tone is left by a leap of a third, and the resolution is by step, some theorists consider the double neighbor a type of cambiata. |

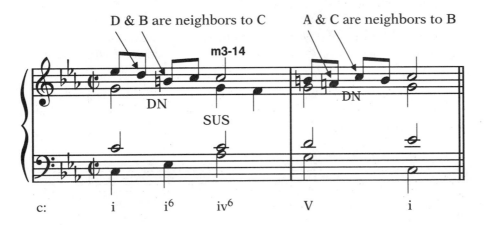

SECOND INVERSION

Cadential I$_4^6$

Triads in second inversion are heard as unstable. They require special attention and should not appear randomly in a chorale-style context. By far the most important second inversion chord is the cadential I$_4^6$. This chord has *no true tonic function*—that is, it doesn't provide any of the sense of rest or repose that an arrival on the tonic normally brings. The cadential I_4^6 is actually part of the dominant function: The bass is the dominant note, and the intervals of the sixth and the fourth above the bass are heard as accented dissonances (appoggiaturas—see under Nonharmonic Tones), resolving to the fifth and the third of the V chord. Cadential I_4^6 therefore directly precedes V, and the sixth and fourth of the I_4^6 must resolve down by step into the fifth and third of V. Since I_4^6–V together have a dominant function, and since I_4^6 has no independent function, but is only a dissonance leading to V, many teachers prefer to label the progression V ($^{6-5}_{4-3}$), with the Arabic numerals showing the voice leading.

Because the sixth and fourth of I_4^6 are accented dissonances, the I_4^6 *chord is accented in relation to V.* Therefore, *cadential I_4^6 must fall on a strong beat,* resolving to V on a weak beat. The sixth and fourth of cadential I_4^6, as dissonances calling for specific resolution, cannot be doubled: double the bass (the dominant).

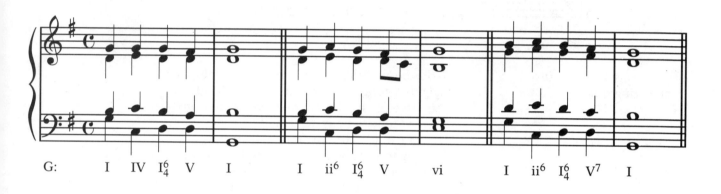

G: I   IV I_4^6 V   I   I   ii^6 I_4^6 V   vi   I   ii^6 I_4^6 V^7 I

Note a common voice leading problem in the progression ii^6–I_4^6. *If the 5th of ii^6 is in the soprano,* and normal doublings are used, there will be a parallel fifth in this progression. This problem is avoided by using a different voicing of ii^6, with the root or third in the soprano. When harmonizing a melody that calls for pre-dominant, then I_4^6 under scale steps $\hat{6}$–$\hat{5}$, use IV instead of ii^6.

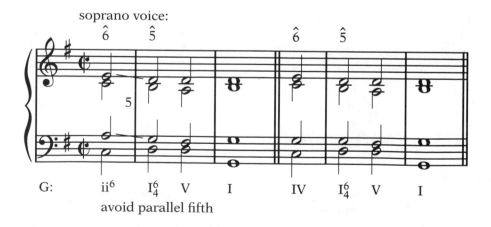

soprano voice: $\hat{6}$ $\hat{5}$ $\hat{6}$ $\hat{5}$

G: ii^6 I_4^6 V   I   IV I_4^6 V   I

avoid parallel fifth

Other Uses of $^6_4$ Inversion

Passing $^6_4$

A passing tone in the bass is harmonized in such a way that a $^6_4$ chord is created. Doubling should promote smoothness; passing $^6_4$ is more likely to appear on a weak beat. Remember: *the bass must be a passing tone—it must get to the $^6_4$ inversion by step and must leave it by step in the same direction.*

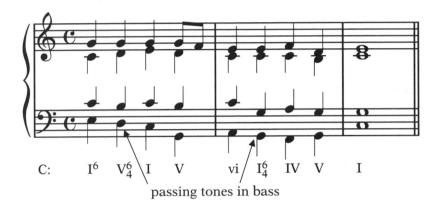

passing tones in bass

Neighbor $^6_4$ or Pedal $^6_4$

Start with a root position triad. With the bass holding, the voices containing the fifth and third of the triad step up (forming a $^6_4$ inversion), then step back. This $^6_4$ chord is not an independent harmony, but rather it simply provides a way of prolonging the original chord. The $^6_4$ is sometimes called "neighbor" because of the movement of the upper voices, and sometimes called "pedal" because the bass holds throughout the pattern.

Arpeggiated $^6_4$

These may occur on weak beats as part of a textural pattern in which root position or first inversion of the same harmony is on the preceding strong beat. An arpeggiated tonic $^6_4$ may also come about in a V–I cadence if the upper parts resolve to I while the bass delays. Note that arpeggiated $^6_4$ chords have no functional independence, and usually receive no Roman numeral label in analysis.

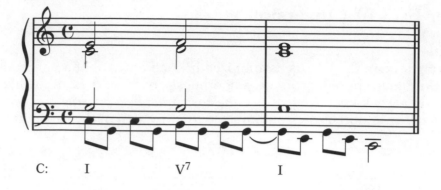

SEVENTH CHORDS

In addition to the root, third, and fifth of a triad, a chord may be extended by adding thirds above the fifth. These are called sevenths, ninths, elevenths, and thirteenths.

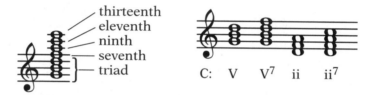

It is easy to see sevenths as added notes, and easy to imagine families of seventh chords as four-note entities, separate from simple triads. But such a view presents an inaccurate picture of sevenths in harmony. In the common practice period, most sevenths in chords come about not as simply added notes, but as nonharmonic tones of one or the other of two specific types. *Most sevenths act as either passing or neighbor tones, or suspensions.* Sevenths almost always *resolve down by step* as the harmony moves.

Dominant Seventh

The **dominant seventh** is a V chord with an added seventh. The seventh typically comes about as a **passing tone,** falling from the doubled root of the V chord, and resolving to the third of the tonic chord. Although the passing motion is typical, the seventh may also arise as a neighbor tone, or may sometimes be an appoggiatura. V^7 is extremely common, and is used in all possible inversions. A closer look at the formation and resolution of each V^7 chord will be found below. Related to the dominant seventh is the $vii°^7$, the full or half diminished seventh chord built on the $vii°$ triad. These are discussed later below.

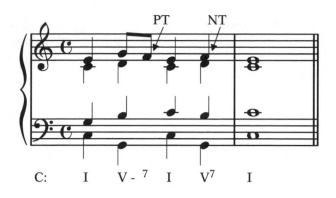

Nondominant Seventh

Seventh chords other than those built on V and vii° are called nondominant seventh chords. The sevenths in these chords almost always come about as suspensions. The most commonly used nondominant sevenths are ii^7 and IV^7, but any triad may include an added seventh as a result of a suspension. See the discussion of ii_5^6 below for a more complete presentation of preparation and resolution of nondominant sevenths.

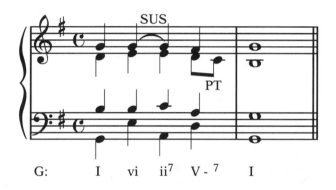

Labeling Seventh Chords in Root Position and in Inversion

Root position chords containing sevenths are labeled with their normal Roman numeral function, followed by a superscript 7: ii^7, V^7, etc.

First inversion seventh chords contain the intervals of 6, 5, and 3 over the bass. These are labeled with Roman numeral functions, and the superscript $_3^6$, or simply $_5^6$: ii_5^6, V_5^6.

Second inversion seventh chords have the intervals of 6, 4, and 3 over the bass. These are labeled as Roman numeral functions with the superscript $_3^6$, or simply $_3^4$: V_3^4, $vii°_3^4$.

Third inversion is a possibility that only arises in chords with four different notes, like seventh chords. In third inversion, the seventh is in the bass, and the intervals over the bass are 6, 4, and 2. These chords are labeled as Roman numeral functions with the superscripts $_2^6$, $_2^4$, or simply 2. For the purposes of labeling, $V_{\frac{6}{\frac{4}{2}}} = V_2^4 = V_2$.

The Dominant Seventh Chord and Its Inversions

Voice leading in resolutions to I given here apply to both major and minor modes.

V^7

Root is in the bass; chord goes to I.

Leading tone resolves to tonic, seventh of chord steps down, fifth also steps down: Resulting I chord has three roots, one third, and no fifth.

C: V^7 I

V^6_5

Leading tone is in the bass, chord goes to I.

Leading tone resolves to tonic, seventh steps down; keep the common tone. Double the root of the I chord.

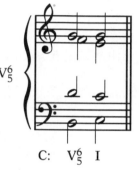

C: V^6_5 I

V^4_3

Fifth of the chord (supertonic of the key) is in bass. Chord goes to I or I^6.

V^4_3-I

Leading tone resolves to tonic, seventh steps down; keep the common tone; root of I is doubled.

$V^4_3-I^6$

Leading tone resolves to tonic, *seventh of chord steps up* (usually), keep common tone. Resulting I chord has a doubled fifth.

If the seventh of V^4_3 descends, as it does in all other resolutions of V^7, the I^6 chord will have a doubled third. This is not impossible, but is much less usual than the doubled fifth resolution.

C: V^4_3 I V^4_3 I^6

Note exception: the seventh steps *up*

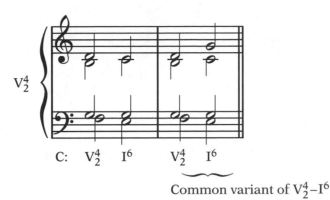

Common variant of V_2^4–I^6

V_2^4

Seventh of chord is in the bass, chord resolves to I^6. Leading tone resolves to tonic, seventh of chord steps down; keep the common tone. I^6 with doubled root results.

A common variant resolves to I^6 with doubled fifth.

FIGURED BASS

Figured bass notation, common in the Baroque period, consists of Arabic numerals (figures) under a conventionally notated bass line. The figures refer to intervals over the bass notes. They provide a shorthand for spelling out harmonies, which the performer interprets and plays.

Triads

In figured bass, 5 or $\frac{5}{3}$ means that the interval of a fifth, or a fifth plus a third, occurs over the given bass note. Since a fifth or fifth-plus-third is characteristic of root position triads, this figure tells us that the chord over the bass note is in root position. If the 5 is standing alone, $\frac{5}{3}$ is understood. If a bass note has no figures below it, root position is usually assumed.

In the same way that 5 or $\frac{5}{3}$ indicates root position, 6 or $\frac{6}{3}$ means first inversion. A 6 standing alone indicates first inversion and $\frac{6}{3}$ is understood. One might think that a 6 standing alone could also suggest $\frac{6}{4}$ or second inversion. But the interval of a fourth is essential to second inversion, and the number 4 is therefore always included in figures indicating $\frac{6}{4}$ inversion. Therefore, $\frac{6}{4}$ = second inversion.

Seventh chords

Using the Arabic numerals to identify intervals above the given bass note, it will be seen that:

$\frac{7}{5}{3}$ means root position seventh chord—can also be shortened to just 7.

$\frac{6}{5}{3}$ means seventh chord in first inversion—can be shortened to $\frac{6}{5}$.

$\frac{6}{4}{3}$ means seventh chord in second inversion—can be shortened to $\frac{4}{3}$.

$\frac{6}{4}{2}$ means seventh chord in third inversion—can be shortened to $\frac{4}{2}$.

Accidentals

Any accidental standing alone under a bass note affects the note a *third above the bass*. A *slash* through any figure indicates that that interval above the bass is raised a half step. Figured bass often includes accidentals next to the figures, which are to be applied to whatever note the figure itself indicates.

Rhythmic Placement

The position of figures within the space of each bar indicates the rhythmic placement of events.

If figures are under a bass attack, the intervals they show will occur along with the bass attack. If the bass has a whole note through a bar, and new figures appear under the middle of the bar, this means that while the bass holds, the upper parts move on the second half note of the bar.

Although figures serve mainly to identify harmony, without indication of voice leading, figures can also express specific melodic or contrapuntal detail, such as passing sevenths and suspensions. In the case of suspensions, the figures give first the dissonance (suspension), then the consonance (resolution) over the bass, and the figures are horizontally aligned to indicate their continuity within in a single voice. Suspension figures are sometimes also connected by a horizontal line. Note again: Spacing of figures tells exactly where in the bar these melodic events occur.

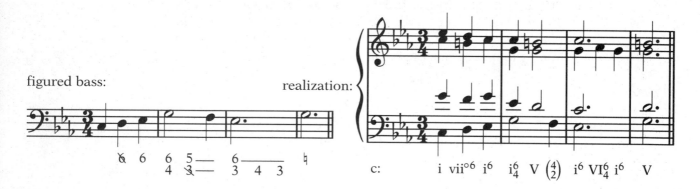

ii$^6_5$

ii$^6_5$ is a ii^7 chord in first inversion. ii^7 is formed by adding a *minor* seventh above the root of the ii triad. Note that the *seventh* of ii^7 is also the *tonic* of the key. This is true whether the ii triad is minor (in major keys) or diminished (in minor keys).

ii$^6_5$ is used in place of ii^6 or IV, to precede V. The added seventh is treated as a *suspension dissonance* (whether or not the seventh is actually tied), with preparation, suspension, and resolution. As you may remember from fourth species, the rhythmic/metric arrangement for suspension dissonance is: preparation on weak beat, suspension on strong beat, resolution on weak beat. Note therefore that correct treatment of ii$^6_5$ involves the chords immediately before and after ii$^6_5$.

Preparation means that the seventh in ii$^6_5$ must come from the same note, in the same voice, in the previous chord. Since the seventh of ii$^6_5$ is the tonic note of the key, the chord before ii$^6_5$ must contain the tonic note as a regular chord tone. This chord will normally fall on a weak beat.

Suspension occurs when the harmony moves from the preparing chord to ii$^6_5$. The seventh of ii$^6_5$ is the suspension. This should occur on a strong beat.

Resolution of the seventh (tonic note of key) is down by step (to the leading tone) as the harmony moves to V. The resolution normally falls on a weak beat.

Note on voice leading from ii$^6_5$ to V: The bass steps up from ii$^6_5$ to V; keep the common tone; the other two upper voices step down from ii$^6_5$ into V.

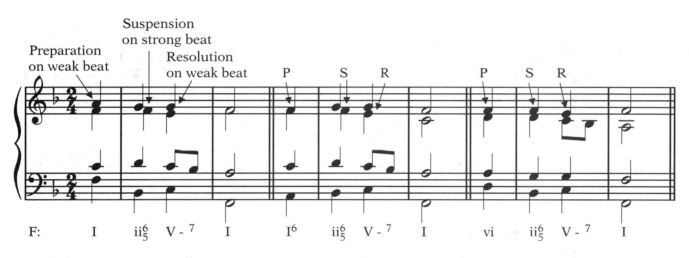

CHROMATICISM—SECONDARY DOMINANTS

Chromaticism may serve to add color or variety to a melody or a harmonic progression, it may provide the suggestion of a harmonic shift, or it may create a complete change in tonal center. All chromaticism in harmony must be understood within the general context of tonal continuity.

Secondary Dominants

A **secondary dominant** is a dominant triad or dominant 7th chord that has as its chord of resolution a triad other than I (or i) in a given key. Any major or minor triad has a dominant 7th that belongs to it, and therefore, the major or minor triad on every scale scale step may be preceded by its own dominant. In C major, for example, the primary V^7 chord is G-B-D-F, but secondary V chords may be formed that resolve to the other triads built on the C-major scale. For example, the ii chord in C major, D-F-A, is a minor triad that has a dominant of its own (Think: What is the dominant of D? The answer is A). The V^7 of the ii chord (D-F-A) is A-C♯-E-G; the V^7 of the iii chord (E-G-B) is B-D♯-F♯-A; the V^7 of the IV chord (F-A-C) is C-E-G-B♭; the V^7 of the V chord (G-B-D) is D-F♯-A-C; the V^7 of the vi chord (A-C-E) is E-G♯-B-D; note that *the vii° chord does not have a secondary dominant:* the vii°

chord is a diminished triad, and therefore could not provide a resolution of a dominant. Following this same logic for the triads of minor keys, one finds that III, IV, V, and VI can have secondary dominants. The ii° chord and the vii° chord are both diminished in minor keys, so they cannot serve as resolutions of secondary dominants.

Secondary dominants (sometimes also called **applied dominants** or **transient dominants**) can occur at any point within the phrase. They very often appear in inversion, especially first inversion. Normally they resolve to the tonic chord they imply, using the regular resolutions of the dominant 7th. In Roman numeral notation, secondary dominants are represented using a slash to stand for the word "of". Thus V/V is read "five of five", V_5^6/ii is read "five six-five of two", and so on. Some examples:

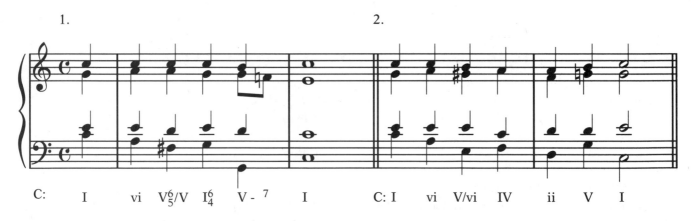

Sometimes secondary dominants resolve irregularly, but these irregular resolutions usually provide either a delayed resolution (1), a form of deceptive cadence (2), or a near resolution in which most of the voices move as expected, often with some added element of chromaticism (3).

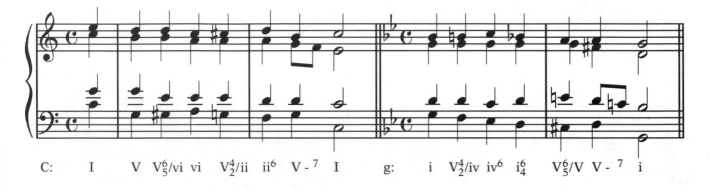

Suppose you are looking at a progression in the key of C major, like this one:

$$\text{C:} \qquad \text{I} \quad \text{vi} \quad ? \quad \text{V} \quad \text{I}$$

What is the third chord? It is a major chord built on the second scale step, leading to V. Is this a II^6? or a V^6/V?

For the answer, look again at the triads derived from the major and minor scales, and review their functions. Remember that triads in the major mode are derived from the major scale, while triads in the minor mode (with the exception of the III chord) are derived from the harmonic minor scale. Below is a table of triads derived from both major and minor modes of the key of C.

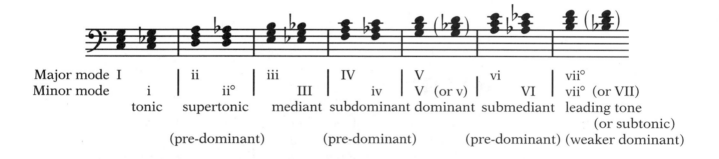

Major mode	I	ii	iii	IV	V	vi	vii°
Minor mode	i	ii°	III	iv	V (or v)	VI	vii° (or VII)
	tonic	supertonic	mediant	subdominant	dominant	submediant	leading tone (or subtonic)
		(pre-dominant)	(pre-dominant)		(pre-dominant)		(weaker dominant)

As you can see, the tonic function is present in both the C-major and c-minor triads; the supertonic function (part of the pre-dominant family) is present in the d-minor and d-diminished triads derived respectively from the major and minor modes. The iii chord of the major mode is a minor triad built on E. The III chord of the minor mode is a major triad built on E flat. Every Roman numeral function has a specific triad derived from each mode.

In terms of Roman numeral function, there is no such thing as a major II chord. The example at the top of the page has a dominant function to the chord that directly follows it, but no independent identity in the key of C. Therefore it should be labeled V^6/V.

Remember that the second, third, sixth, and seventh scale steps in major do not generate major triads. The major triads III, VI, and VII are based on scale steps found only in the minor mode. Major triads built on the second, third, sixth, and seventh scale steps of major scales function as secondary dominants. In example 1, each segment shows first a triad in G major, then the corresponding triad in g minor, then the secondary dominant built from the major-mode scale step.

Realize also that a major triad takes on a new identity when a minor 7th is added to it. For this reason, the chord in example 2, below, is labeled V^7/IV—not I^7.

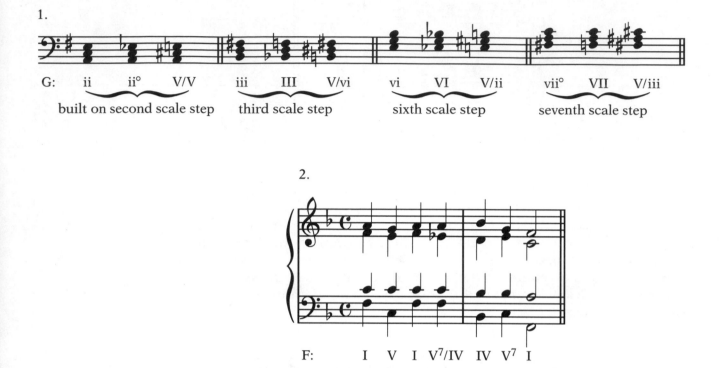

1.

G: ii   ii°   V/V   iii   III   V/vi   vi   VI   V/vii   vii°   VII   V/iii

  built on second scale step   third scale step   sixth scale step   seventh scale step

2.

F: I   V   I   V^7/IV   IV   V^7 I

TONICIZATION

The term **tonicization** implies the potential for a new tonic. In a tonicization, a secondary dominant and its resolution form the *cadence* of a phrase. The scale degree of this cadence is said to be "tonicized": It has the potential of becoming a new tonic. If a new tonic is confirmed in the next phrase, that is, if the music has actually changed key, this is a *modulation*. A discussion of modulation begins on page 63.

Very often, after a tonicization, the music's continuation does not confirm a move to a new tonic. Instead, the next phrase continues on in the old tonic. This is a typical situation in Bach chorales. There the cadences, if not full, half, or deceptive, are usually tonicizations. True modulations are rare in chorales. Notice in the example below that chromatic passing tones smooth the way for the tonicizations of V in measures 2 and 4. Note also that V/V in measure 2 is preceded by its own ii$^6_5$ chord.

Wie schön leuchtet der Morgenstern

J. S. Bach

Tonicizations often include more than just a secondary dominant and resolution at a cadence point. Frequently several chords preceding the cadence are best understood as belonging to the tonicized key (although after the cadence the music still returns to the original key). In these situations, labeling Roman numerals using a bracket to indicate the secondary key makes the analysis clear. Note that while tonicizations are usually full cadences, they can also be half cadences (i.e., cadences on V of some key other than that of the prevailing tonic).

DIMINISHED SEVENTH CHORDS

The vii°⁷ chord is built up from the leading tone in ascending minor thirds. Although its pitches are drawn from the minor mode, vii°⁷ is used freely in major as well as minor contexts. vii°⁷ is an unstable sonority that requires resolution to the tonic. Its function is comparable to that of a dominant, but weaker than a dominant for two reasons: 1) vii°⁷ is built on the diminished triad, lacks a stabilizing perfect fifth, and is symmetrical; its sonority is the same whether in root position or any inversion; and 2) all the notes of vii°⁷ act as neighbors to notes in the tonic chord, so that there is no distinctive bass pattern comparable to that of a V–I progression.

In resolving vii°⁷ to I, it is helpful to think of vii°⁷ as two pairs of tritones. In the example below G♯-D and B-F are the tritone pairs. In general you should follow this rule in resolving vii°⁷ to I:

A diminished 5th resolves *in* to a third.

An augmented 4th resolves *out* to a sixth.

Note in the example that different voicings of vii°⁷ produce different intervals (d5 or A4) and therefore different voicings of the resolving i chord.

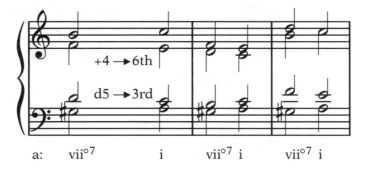

Another way to think of the normal resolution—if vii°⁷ is spelled in order from the bottom, normally the lower two notes step up while the upper two step down.

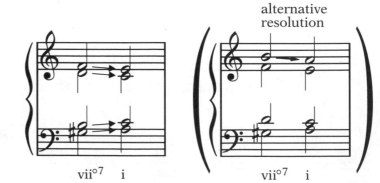

Note: 1) all voices of vii°⁷ move *by step* into i; 2) the resulting i chord has a *doubled third;* and 3) a frequently seen variation involves moving the third of vii°⁷ down to the tonic to give a doubled root to the i chord (see example in bracket above).

Inversions of vii°⁷

vii°$^6_5$ = first inversion of vii°⁷. vii°$^4_3$ = second inversion. vii°$^4_2$ = third inversion. Because vii°⁷ consists of four minor thirds (which evenly divide the octave), there is no difference *in sonority* between root position and inversions. In order to correctly analyze a vii°⁷ or its inversion, you must 1) check the spelling and 2) check the chord of resolution.

In the following example there are three vii°⁷ chords with different spellings. Each of these chords sounds exactly like the other two. Their key orientation can only be *heard* when they resolve. The spelling of each vii°⁷ chord uses the appropriate accidentals for the key of resolution. In each case the voice leading follows the rule already stated:

Diminished 5ths resolve *in* to thirds. Augmented 4ths resolve *out* to sixths.

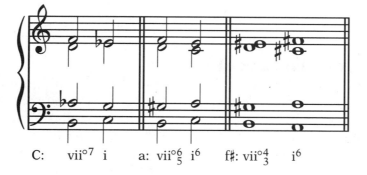

C: vii°⁷ i   a: vii°$^6_5$ i⁶   f♯: vii°$^4_3$ i⁶

Here are some examples of vii°⁷ and inversions with normal resolutions. Tritones are resolved according to the rule stated above except in the case of vii°$^6_5$-i. The usual movement of the tritones would require vii°$^6_5$ to resolve to i⁶. Quite frequently, however, vii°$^6_5$ resolves to i (root position) instead. In this case, the bass note and its tritone (diminished 5th) move in parallel motion to a perfect 5th instead of converging to a third. This diminished to perfect 5th is best avoided in outer voices, but is not considered a parallel 5th.

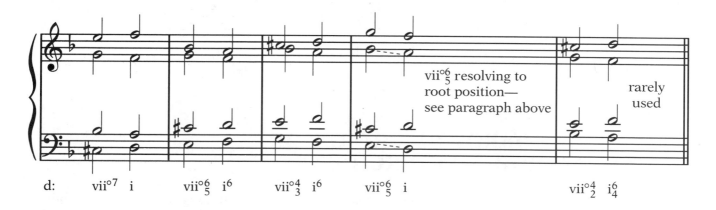

vii°$^6_5$ resolving to root position— see paragraph above

rarely used

d: vii°⁷ i   vii°$^6_5$ i⁶   vii°$^4_3$ i⁶   vii°$^6_5$ i   vii°$^4_2$ i$^6_4$

vii°⁷ resolves to i or I just as V resolves to i or I. In the context of a progression we often see secondary dominants, and in the same way, we can now recognize *secondary diminished-7th chords*. When a chord other than the tonic is preceded by its own vii°⁷, this is a secondary vii°⁷. Secondary vii°⁷ chords (and inversions) are spelled according to the key to which they belong. They generally resolve with completely normal voice leading and resolution of tritones. A common exception to normal voice leading is vii°⁷/V–V. In this case the doubled third, which is normal in the resolution of vii°⁷, is avoided so as not to double the leading tone in V.

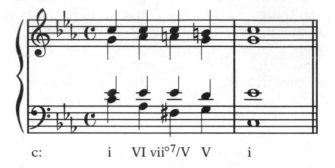

c: i   VI vii°⁷/V V   i

Half-Diminished Seventh

The half-diminished 7th (vii°⁷) is a variant of vii°⁷ (full-diminished). It is derived from the major scale and consists of a diminshed triad built on the leading tone, plus a *minor seventh over the root;* (the full-diminished seventh consists of a diminished leading tone triad, plus a *diminished seventh over the root*). In Roman numeral labeling, a circle superscript with a line through it indicates half-diminished. Like full vii°⁷, the half-diminished vii°⁷ is a neighbor chord to the tonic. All voices should move by step to the resolution. The tritone should resolve as described above. Take care that the other two voices do not move in parallel 5ths.

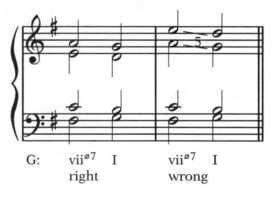

G: vii°⁷   I   vii°⁷   I
        right   wrong

BORROWED CHORDS OR MODAL INTERCHANGE

The chart on page 53 shows all the triads that belong to the key of C, both major and minor modes. It is helpful to conceive of keys as embracing all the triads of both modes, because composers throughout the common practice period have often made use of harmonies "borrowed" from one mode or the other. This use of borrowed chords is called mode mixture or modal interchange. A familiar example is the Picardy third, in which a major I chord provides tonic function at the cadence for a phrase (or a whole piece) that has been in minor mode. Other than the Picardy third, instances of mode mixture are more likely to involve chords borrowed from the minor mode that are used in a prevailingly major mode context.

When analyzing triads, use the Roman numeral symbol that is appropriate for the function and chord quality of every triad. Accidentals always have some analytical explanation: They are part of the minor mode; they create borrowed chords; they belong to secondary dominants; or they are chromatic nonharmonic tones. Accidentals may also signal a change of key. This topic is taken up below.

A few examples of borrowed chords:

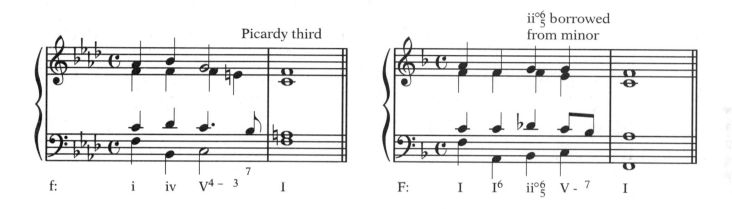

iv and ii°⁶ borrowed from minor

Deceptive cadence to VI borrowed from minor mode—this VI is often called "flat six," and labeled ♭VI

NEAPOLITAN TRIAD AND NEAPOLITAN SIXTH

A chromatically altered ii chord, the Neapolitan triad is a major triad built on the chromatically lowered second scale degree. For example, in the key of C, Neapolitan = D♭-F-A♭; in B♭, Neapolitan = C♭-E♭-G♭; in F♯, Neapolitan = G-B-D, etc.

The Neapolitan triad in a given key has more in common with the minor mode than with the major, and it is seen somewhat more frequently in minor contexts. In can be used with either mode, however, and the notes contained in the Neapolitan triad are the same whether the prevailing mode is major or minor.

The Neapolitan triad is almost always presented in first inversion, and is therefore usually called Neapolitan sixth, abbreviated N⁶ or ♭II⁶. N⁶ functions as a pre-dominant: it moves to V (or i₄⁶-V). In terms of doubling and voice leading, it is identical to ii⁶ moving to V: The bass note is doubled. As the bass steps up to V, the three upper parts all move down to the closest note in the V chord. Note the interval of a diminished third that occurs in one voice as N⁶ moves to V. This is accepted as a normal part of this progression. When N⁶ moves to i₄⁶, all three upper voices step down against the rising bass.

Examples:

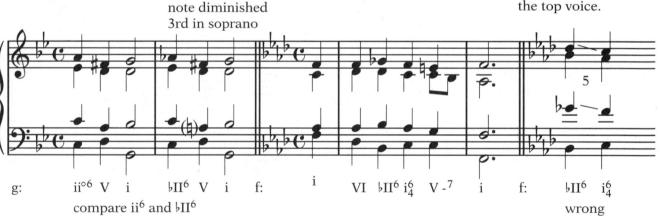

note diminished
3rd in soprano

avoid parallel 5ths as ♭II⁶ moves to I₄⁶; don't put the fifth of ♭II⁶ in the top voice.

g: ii°⁶ V i   ♭II⁶ V i   f: i   VI ♭II⁶ i₄⁶ V -⁷   i   f: ♭II⁶ i₄⁶

compare ii⁶ and ♭II⁶   wrong

AUGMENTED SIXTH CHORDS

This is a group of three chords with pre-dominant function, all of which are derived from iv⁶. The progression augmented 6th–V is a chromatically intensified iv⁶–V (Phrygian cadence) progression. In the example, compare the pitches of iv⁶ to the three basic pitches of all three augmented 6th chords: iv⁶ contains the minor sixth scale

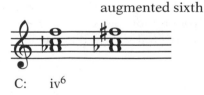

augmented sixth

C: iv⁶

degree in the bass, the tonic note, and the fourth scale step; all augmented 6th chords contain the minor sixth scale degree (virtually always as the bass), the tonic note, and the *chromatically raised fourth scale degree*. The chromatically raised fourth creates the interval of an augmented sixth over the bass, giving the chord its name. The raised fourth functions as a leading tone to the dominant.

In addition to the minor sixth scale step in the bass, tonic note, and raised fourth scale step, one more note is needed. The specific identity of this last note determines the specific name of each of the three augmented 6th chords:

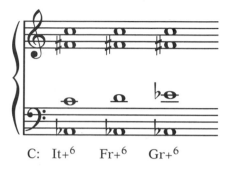

Italian 6th: (label It+6)
minor sixth scale step in bass, tonic, raised 4th + doubling of tonic note

French 6th: (label Fr+6)
minor sixth scale step in bass, tonic, raised 4th + second scale degree

German 6th: (label Gr+6)
minor sixth scale step in bass, tonic, raised 4th + minor third scale step

Augmented 6th chords resolve to V in root position. The minor sixth scale step in the bass has a very strong tendency to settle down on the dominant. The raised fourth scale degree resolves up to the dominant. Voice leading keeps any common tones, with all other voices moving by step. All three augmented 6th chords may go to i$^6_4$ and then V. This pattern is especially common for the German 6th, since going through i$^6_4$ eliminates the parallel 5ths that result if the German 6th moves directly to V. It should be noted that these parallel 5ths are not considered incorrect—they are often seen in music literature.

Augmented 6th chords have more in common with minor than with major mode, but they can be used in either major or minor context. In either mode, ALWAYS CHECK ACCIDENTALS CAREFULLY WHEN WRITING OR ANALYZING AUGMENTED SIXTH CHORDS!!

Examples:

OTHER DIMINISHED SEVENTH CHORDS— #ii°⁷ AND #vi°⁷

There are two frequently seen diminished 7th chords that are not built on a leading tone and don't have the dominant-related function that vii°⁷ chords do. There is no clear agreement on a name for these chords; some names that teachers use for these are **common tone diminished chords, appoggiatura diminished chords,** and **neighbor diminished chords.**

These chords come from the major mode, although they occasionally appear in minor mode contexts. They are built on the second scale step, chromatically raised, and on the the sixth scale step (from major), also chromatically raised. In C major, these chords are built on d♯ and a♯. In F major they are built on g♯ and d♯. In A-flat major they are built on b and on f♯. Like all diminished 7th chords, these consist entirely of stacked minor thirds. There is no clear consensus on the Roman numeral labeling of these chords, since they relate only to the chord of resolution they directly precede, and yet are not secondary diminished 7th (i.e., leading tone) chords. Because of their spelling, we will call them #ii°⁷ ("raised two diminished"), and #vi°⁷ (raised six diminished). In a key where the second or sixth scale step is flat, these chords will be labeled ♮ii°⁷ and ♮vi°⁷. Here are some examples.

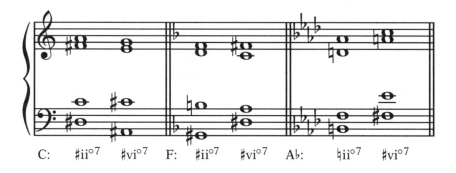

Resolution

#ii°⁷ resolves to I⁶, as shown below. #vi°⁷ resolves to V⁶₄. Note that the resolutions keep the common tone while the other voices move by step. Both chords can be inverted, still resolving with a common tone and the other voices moving by step. In analysis, watch for misspellings of these chords!

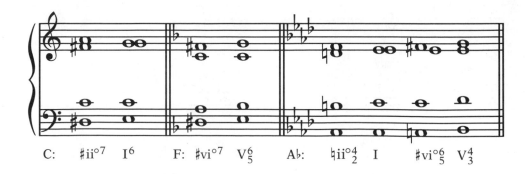

Try these progressions:

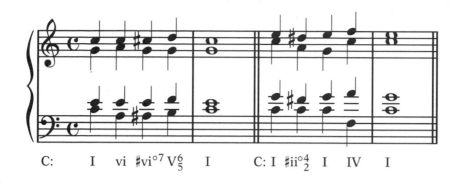

C: I   vi ♯vi°⁷ V⁶₅   I   C:I ♯ii°⁴₂ I IV   I

MODULATION

Modulation means a change of key. In a modulation, all the functional relationships of the original scale are changed: one hears a new tonic, a new dominant functioning toward that tonic, and so on. A modulation begins with a tonicization of some sort. That is, the potential of a new key is suggested at a cadence point. The difference between a tonicization and a modulation lies in what happens after this cadence. In a tonicization, the music begins the next phrase in the original key. In a modulation, the next phrase confirms the move to a new key. A modulation is therefore a stronger move away from the tonic than a tonicization. A modulation can be quite long and elaborate, and can require a series of additional key changes to come back to the original key.

In order for a modulation to sound smooth in the ongoing continuity of tonal harmony, it must come about through the use of something shared between the old key and the new one. Whatever is shared contitutes the **pivot** of a modulation.

Pivot Chord

The shared element in a modulation may be a single note or a melodic fragment, but most often there is some shared harmony between the old key and the new. A shared chord or chord progession can be analyzed in either key. It constitutes a "gray area" between the two keys which allows the modulation to seem gradual and smooth.

The pivot chord is a shared chord between two keys in a modulation. It is never the dominant of the new key, because that chord belongs entirely to the new key. Therefore, the pivot chord comes before the new dominant in a modulation. Frequently there are several potential pivot chords (a "gray area") in a modulating passage, and one might correctly say that they all create the effect of pivoting from one key to the other. In general, the pivot chord or chords are labeled as in the example below. Make sure that they precede the new dominant, and that Roman numerals (not note names) are used to label them. In this way the analysis shows exactly what is heard: a stable initial key; an ambiguous chord or progression that can be heard as having specific function in the first key, but can also be interpreted as functional in the new key; a new key established that has a specific relationship to the old one.

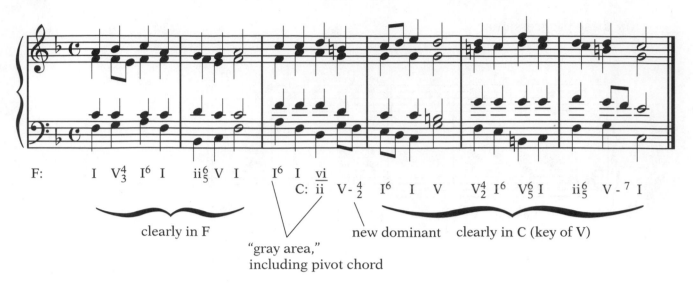

While there are modulations that do not have pivot chords (they may have pivotal pitches, may involve melodic bridges, or may be purposely abrupt), there is no standard way of labeling these. The vast majority of modulations use some sort of pivot chords. Note that secondary dominants, secondary diminished 7ths, modal interchange, and enharmonic relationships can be used to expand the possibilities of pivot chords.

Large-Scale Harmonic Structure

A modulation can link any two keys. What makes a composer choose one key over another? There are many answers to this question, including some relatively subjective factors such as individual taste and expressive intent. But there are also more objective criteria, including large-scale structure and the degree of relationship between keys.

The large-scale harmonic motion of works in the common practice period tends to reflect the familiar small-scale patterns of the tonal language. Thus the simplest and most common tonal relationship, I - V - I, is, on the largest scale, the harmonic outline of the vast majority of tonal pieces in major keys. These pieces begin in the tonic, modulate to the dominant, and then come back to the tonic at the end. A similar outline is seen in minor mode pieces. Here, the first move tends to be to the relative major, then to the dominant, then home to the tonic (i - III; V - i).

The fact that so many pieces share basic structures is part of the coherence of the tonal language, but it does not tell us anything about each piece's unique characteristics. For this, a more detailed analysis is needed. On the structural level, a longer piece may go through many keys, especially coming back from a modulation to the dominant. It is always helpful to make a structural diagram of the key areas of longer pieces, showing their succession as a Roman numeral progression. It may take some practice to *hear* on this large scale, but the effort will pay dividends in the understanding of form.

Closely Related Keys

The notion of keys as more closely or more distantly related is helpful in understanding harmonic structure. Think for a moment of a key as represented by its scale. The process of modulation can be understood as the introduction of accidentals. When we modulate from C major to G major, we introduce an f-sharp and eliminate the f-natural. This is a relatively easy modulation to make smoothly, because the change involves only one note. It is much more difficult to modulate to F-sharp major, which has only one note in common with C major.

Keys are related according to the number of notes they have in common. Keys are considered closely related to other keys one accidental away on the circle of fifths. Thus a key with two sharps is considered closely related to keys with one sharp and to keys with three sharps, as well as to its own relative, which shares its two-sharp key signature. In other words, D major is closely related to e minor, G major, f-sharp minor, A major and b minor. Look at these keys and compare them to the triads of the key of D major:

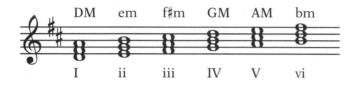

As you can see, all the major and minor triads of the key of D major are the tonic triads of the closely related keys.

Compare b minor and its closely related keys: Once again, observe that all the major and minor triads of the key are the tonic triads of the closely related keys.

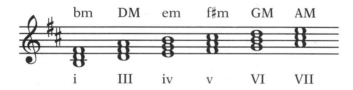

Tonal pieces tend to modulate to closely related keys. However, more remote modulations are also possible and seen increasingly from the middle of the nineteenth century into the twentieth.

SUGGESTIONS FOR ANALYSIS AND FURTHER READING

Analysis

Any common practice period music can be studied for harmonic analysis, and the utility and pleasure of studying scores go hand in hand as skill develops. A good anthology is especially helpful for students and there are several available. Particularly recommended is the *Anthology for Musical Analysis* (5th ed.) by Charles Burkhart (Holt, Rinehart and Winston, 1994). Students (and teachers) sometimes mistakenly believe that Bach chorales are the best elementary pieces for harmonic analysis, because of their clear four-part format. Chorales make fine pieces for study, but they can be quirky and difficult both because of the modal origins of many of the tunes, and because of the complexity of the part writing. Works from the classic period are often more straightforward harmonically.

Further Reading

There are a great many texts that cover harmony, and many of these are valuable. One of the best known and most widely used twentieth-century texts is *Harmony* by Walter Piston, now updated and expanded by Mark DeVoto (W. W. Norton). Those looking for a more contrapuntal approach might try *Harmony and Voice Leading* by Edward Aldwell and Carl Schachter (Harcourt Brace Jovanovich). In addition to Piston, a number of other significant twentieth-century composers have written textbooks on common practice period theory, including Paul Hindemith, Arnold Schoenberg, and Roger Sessions.

PART 4
Tonal Counterpoint

Tonal counterpoint, also called eighteenth-century counterpoint or Baroque-style counterpoint, is related to species counterpoint (see Part 2), but with several important differences. First of all, a study of tonal counterpoint must be based on actual music from the eighteenth and nineteenth centuries; tonal counterpoint was not developed as a teaching tool, and it does not have any basic text that lays out its rules and procedures, as Fux's *Gradus ad Parnassum* does for species counterpoint. On the contrary, the "rules" of tonal counterpoint, like those of harmony, are derived from a huge body of musical literature. Secondly, techniques of tonal counterpoint are related to those learned in species in terms of consonance and dissonance, but with one crucial addition—in tonal counterpoint the underlying frame of reference at all times (playing a role similar to that of the cantus firmus in species counterpoint) is harmonic progression. Thus the study of tonal counterpoint combines the harmonic materials presented in the previous unit with the kind of linear considerations first introduced in Part 2.

We tend to associate the idea of tonal counterpoint with formal types from the Baroque period, such as inventions, fugues, chorale preludes, etc. Some of these involve special techniques, such as imitation, and some have particular tonal patterns. These special techniques and patterns will be discussed below. Canons, rounds, and fugues are discussed in some detail in this section, because the techniques involved come up often in analysis. Other common contrapuntal forms are discussed briefly in the section on form.

The study of counterpoint cannot be restricted to contrapuntal forms. While these forms feature counterpoint throughout, contrapuntal textures appear at some point in most works of the common practice period. Moreover, the movement of individual voices, even in homophonic music, creates a form of counterpoint. Therefore the general techniques of tonal counterpoint are essentially inseparable from the study of tonal music.

The following discussion of tonal counterpoint is not a complete study of this subject. Its purpose is to provide an overview of the topic with enough information to be of practical use for writing and analysis within the context of general theory studies.

MELODIC LINE

Melodic Line: Intervals

There are no special rules that govern intervals in the melodic line. In species counterpoint augmented and diminished intervals are specifically avoided because they tend to split the line into different registers. In tonal counterpoint these intervals are frequently used precisely to take advantage of this property. In example 1a, below, the melodic line contains both a diminished 7th and a tritone. These two intervals (helped also by the large leap on the downbeat of the second measure) divide the line into two separate registers, giving the illusion of two lines within a single melody. In example 1b, these two lines are separated by beaming; the upper voice notes are all beamed together above, while those of the lower voice are all beamed together below. Each of these two lines moves essentially by step.

Note that most of the larger intervals involve **tendency tones:** the leading tone needs to resolve up to the tonic, and the lowered sixth scale step needs to move down to the dominant. These tendencies are important in shaping the line and giving it direction. Tendency tones do not necessarily need to resolve immediately. Skipping away from the leading tone on beat 3, measure 1, creates a sense of unfinished business that the melody responds to and ultimately resolves in measure 2.

In example 2, the same basic melody is presented in harmonized form. Some of the melody's "lower voice" has now become the bass line (dotted lines and arrows show where these connections are). Note that the large leaps of the original melody (on beat three of measure 1 and beats one and two of measure 2) are **arpeggiations** of the harmony. Note also the melody contains *nonharmonic tones* (the passing tones, labeled PT, at the beginning and end).

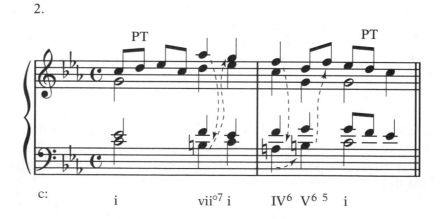

From these examples we can make some general observations that apply to melodic lines in this style:

- A melodic line has harmonic implications.
- All intervals are possible, as are large leaps; but pitches in the melodic line are generally either chord-tones (i.e., they belong to the

implied harmony) or are treated as nonharmonic tones (passing, neighbor, suspension, anticipation, échappée, cambiata, or appoggiatura dissonances).

- Tendency tones are melodically resolved (they move to more stable tones according to their tendencies), but not always immediately.

Melodic Shape and Cadence Patterns

All cadences that are common in tonal music (full, half, deceptive, Phrygian, plagal) are used in contrapuntal textures. The lessons learned in species counterpoint apply much more generally here: Melodies tend to build to a high point and descend gradually to a final cadence on the tonic. This may occur over the course of a phrase, but may also occur over the course of several phrases or an entire piece. Intermediate cadences may come to rest on any note, depending upon the shape and direction of the line and the implied harmony. A final melodic cadence will usually supply the tonic note. In a top voice, the tonic is generally delivered either literally by step (as in species cadences), or essentially by step, with some decorative arpeggiation breaking up the direct line (see example 3a). A final cadence in the bass line will usually go from the fifth scale step to the tonic (i.e., V-I), as in example 3b.

3a.

3b.

C:

C:

TWO-PART COUNTERPOINT

Much of the technique learned in connection with species counterpoint also applies to two-part tonal counterpoint: The classification of *consonance and dissonance* and the prohibition against obvious **parallel 5ths and 8ves** remain the same. In general, dissonances should be identifiable as nonharmonic tones.

   Direct fifths and octaves, which are clearly regulated in species counterpoint, are more ambiguous in tonal counterpoint. These require judgment: If they sound too much like parallels, they should be eliminated. This is especially likely if they are approached by leap in both parts (examples 4a and 4b). But if they are not too conspicuous (usually if one voice steps while the other leaps), or if they come about in a V-I cadence at the end of a phrase, they can be quite acceptable (example 4c). "**Horn fifths**" are commonly used (example 4d). In horn fifths, the upper part moves in scale steps $\hat{3}$-$\hat{2}$-$\hat{1}$ while the bass moves I-V-I⁶. The reverse pattern ($\hat{1}$-$\hat{2}$-$\hat{3}$, I⁶-V-I) is also called horn fifths. These patterns derive their name from typical writing for natural horns. The direct fifths contained in these patterns are considered perfectly correct in two-part counterpoint.

4a.
no—direct 8ve
by large leaps

4b.
no—direct 5th by leaps
(and parallel 5th)

4c.
yes—direct 8ve
at cadence,
one voice by step

4d.
yes—horn fifths

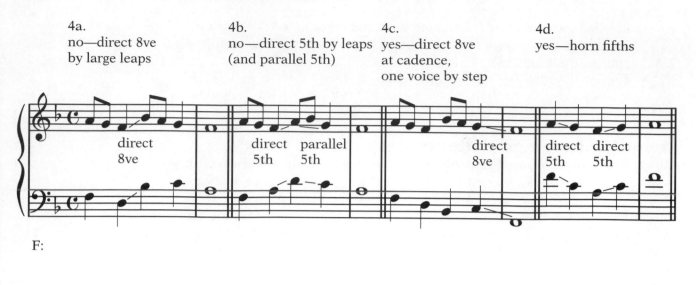

F:

To begin writing two-part tonal counterpoint, take a simple chord progression, such as that in example 5:

5.

C: I   I⁶   ii⁶   V-⁷   I

Leaving the bass line as it is, it is possible to invent an upper-part counterpoint using the progression as an outline for arpeggiations, and making use
of nonharmonic tones. Example 6 shows some of the possibilities.

6a.   6b.

C:

6c.   6d.

Contrapuntal Texture
Unequal rhythmic values
The examples above all use faster note values over the steady quarters of the bass. But it is also possible to let the bass move more quickly than the upper part, choosing the extra bass notes carefully, so as not to obscure the harmonic progression. In example 7a, beat 1 contains an added passing tone, while beats 2, 3, and 4 all arpeggiate on the weak eighth. Example 7b combines the elaborated bass line with one of the melodies derived from the previous example. Here both parts move at more or less the same pace. Every note in each part can still be understood as a chord tone or a nonharmonic tone.

7a.   7b.

C:

Distinct melodic contours
When both voices move at the same pace, the melodic contours of the two parts should be different if a contrapuntal effect is desired. If the parts move in parallel motion, the contrapuntal effect is minimized (example 8). Parallel motion is not always a flaw, however. On the contrary, composers have often used passages in parallel motion to provide contrast in overall contrapuntal works. Parallel 3rds, 6ths, 10ths, etc. are all acceptable.

8.

G:

Bass line arpeggiations

The techniques used in elaborating the bass line into a more complex or faster-moving part are the same as those used for an upper part. Arpeggiations and nonharmonic tones supply the extra notes. A complication in this general procedure may arise when the bass line arpeggiates to the fifth of a root position or first inversion harmony. Sometimes the fifth may be strong enough to make the harmony sound like a true *six-four chord* rather than an elaboration. Genuine six-four chords need to have cadential, passing, or neighbor (pedal) function in counterpoint, just as they do in harmony (see page 43), and they should not be used randomly.

Example 9 starts again with the basic chord progression. In the eighth-note version of the bass line, the fifth on beat 1 is possible because it comes on the weak eighth, and because beats 1 and 2 together still project a root position I chord. But on beat 3 the fifth of the ii chord is not acceptable because it occurs as the strong part of the beat, because the harmonic function is not clear at the time it occurs, and because of the accented perfect 4th it forms with the melody. As with species counterpoint, on-the-beat perfect 4ths are avoided in two-voice textures, unless one of the parts is a clearly functioning dissonance that is properly resolved.

9.

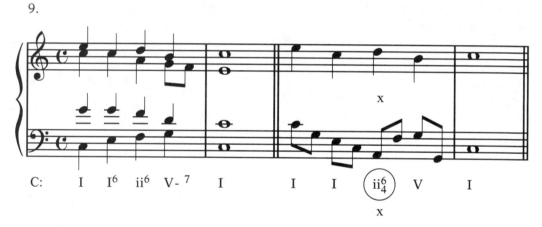

C: I   I⁶   ii⁶   V– ⁷   I   I   I   (ii⁶₄)   V   I

Chromaticism is as common in counterpoint as it is in all tonal music. As in harmony, chromatic alterations arise from one of four sources: raising and lowering of the sixth and seventh scale steps of the melodic minor scale; chromatic passing or neighbor tones; secondary dominants in the harmonic progression; and modulation. In both writing and analysis, any chromaticism should fall into one of these categories, and care should be taken in writing to resolve any chromatically altered notes according to their tendencies. Example 10 illustrates chromaticism (except for modulation).

10.

c: i   V⁶   i   V⁶   i   VI   V⁶₅/V   V

INVERTIBLE COUNTERPOINT IN TWO VOICES

Invertibility in a two-voice texture means that either part can serve as upper or lower voice. Invertible counterpoint between two voices is also called **double counterpoint**. If the lower voice is transposed up an octave, and becomes a plausible upper counterpoint to the original upper voice, this is called **invertibility at the octave** or **inversion at the octave**.[*]

Obviously, a similar effect will be achieved if the the lower voice stays in position and the upper voice transposes down an octave. If one of the voices moves by two octaves, or if each voice moves by an octave in order to trade places, the result is *invertibility or inversion at the fifteenth* (example 11a). Invertible counterpoint exists with relationships other than the octave (or fifteenth). Such counterpoint is classified according to the total amount of displacement involved for both voices, for example, *double counterpoint at the tenth* (example 11b) *or at the twelfth* (example 11c). Extra octaves of displacement are not figured into this naming system. For example, invertibility at a tenth plus an octave is still referred to as invertibility at the tenth, not at the seventeenth.

Invertible Counterpoint at the Fifteenth
Upper part moves down an octave, lower part up an octave:

11a.

G:

---

[*] It is important not to confuse the idea of invertible counterpoint, which involves the relative positioning of two (or more) voices, with the idea of *melodic inversion*. In melodic inversion, each interval of a line is mirrored, so that a step up becomes a step down, a fifth down becomes a fifth up, and so on. This technique is sometimes used in contrapuntal textures (see Imitation and Canon and Fugue, below).

Invertible Counterpoint at the Tenth
Upper part moves down an octave, lower part moves up a third:

11b.

C:

Invertible Counterpoint at the Twelfth
Upper part moves down an octave, lower part moves up a fifth:

11c.

C:

Double counterpoint at the octave or fifteenth is commonly used in contrapuntal textures throughout the common practice period, and invertibility at the tenth or twelfth, while less common, is sometimes seen. Double counterpoint at other intervals is quite rare.

For two lines that are invertible at the octave or the fifteenth, what happens to each vertical interval when the parts are exchanged? An octave will remain an octave (or fifteenth); a second inverts to a seventh and vice versa, a third inverts to a sixth and vice versa, a fifth inverts to a fourth and a fourth to a fifth. Tritones invert to tritones (example 12).

For invertible counterpoint at the octave or fifteenth:

12.

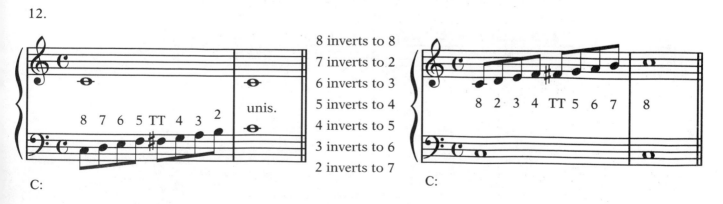

8 inverts to 8
7 inverts to 2
6 inverts to 3
5 inverts to 4
4 inverts to 5
3 inverts to 6
2 inverts to 7

Since both seconds and sevenths are dissonances in two voices, they will not be used except as passing tones, neighbor tones, etc., in which case they will continue to function when the lines are inverted. A tritone that resolves properly to a third or sixth will also resolve correctly when inverted. Thirds, sixths, and octaves are all acceptable in two voices, and so can all be inverted at the octave. The only problematic interval for octave inversion is the fifth: A fifth is perfectly correct in two voices, but if the parts are inverted at the octave, the perfect 5th becomes a perfect 4th. Perfect 4ths are dissonant in two-voice counterpoint and must be avoided except as functioning dissonances. From this it should be clear why invertible counterpoint at the octave or fifteenth relies almost completely on thirds, sixths, and octaves, and avoids perfect 5ths. In example 13a, below, the fifths are completely acceptable, but in example 13b, showing the two parts inverted, the fourths are errors.

13a.   13b.

C:

IMITATION AND CANON

The examples above create counterpoint between two voices by giving each voice a separate rhythmic identity, or by making a different contour in each part. Another common contrapuntal texture is **imitation.** In imitation, one voice copies the other. If the imitation is exact (intervalically the same, starting on the same pitch or transposed), and if this imitative relationship lasts through the whole piece, the piece is a **canon.**

The most familiar type of canon is the **round** (also called a **circle canon** or **perpetual canon**, because the parts can be repeated without end). Canons that cannot repeat, but are simply performed once through to the cadence are classified according to the intervalic relationship between the voices, such as canon at the octave, canon at the fifth, and so on (for a canon at some interval other than the octave or unison, the second voice usually adjusts so as to imitate the first within a diatonic framework). In a canon, the first voice is sometimes referred to by the Latin name **dux** (leader) and the imitating voice is called the **comes** (follower).

A simple round, such as *Row, Row, Row Your Boat* (example 14) relies on harmonic stasis to control the chord progression: The entire round is essentially on the tonic chord.

14.

C:

A more developed example, such as *White Choral Bells* (example 15) illustrates the basic technique of harmonic control in a canon. Here the *comes* enters at the beginning of the third bar. Therefore, measures 3 and 1 must match harmonically, beat by beat, and measures 2 and 4 must also match. The clear direction of each half of this tune helps the overall melodic flow.

15.

There are several more complex canonic types, including the following: If the rhythmic values in the *comes* are proportionally longer than those in the *dux* (a half note in the *comes* answers a quarter note in the *dux*, for instance), the result is a **canon in augmentation**. If the rhythmic values of the *comes* are proportionally shorter than those of the *dux* (e.g., an eighth note in the *comes* answers a quarter note in the *dux*), the result is a **canon in diminution**. If the *comes* plays the *dux* backwards, a **canon in retrograde** results. This technique is also called a **crab canon** or *canon cancrizans*. If the *comes* duplicates each interval of the *dux*, but with the *direction* of the interval reversed (i.e., *melodic inversion*: the *dux* begins with a perfect 4th up, so the *comes* begins with a perfect 4th down, etc.), the result is a **canon in inversion**. Canons may involve more than two voices, and canonic pieces may also include one or more accompanying free voices.

Although many canons exist in renaissance and Baroque literature, the device of canon is only a small corner of the study of counterpoint. Imitation that is brief in duration and/or inexact intervalically is much more common than canon as a contrapuntal texture. The examples below show imitation at the octave and at the fifth as they might occur in the noncanonic part of ongoing contrapuntal textures.

Imitation at the octave:

16a.

c:

Imitation at the fifth:

16b.

Bb:

The Baroque period saw the rise of tonal counterpoint, and works featuring imitation abound in that period. Good examples of noncanonic but generally imitative counterpoint are the *Two-Part Inventions* and *Three-Part Inventions* (also called *Sinfonias*) of J. S. Bach.

COUNTERPOINT IN THREE OR MORE PARTS

Three-voice textures are extremely common in contrapuntal writing, because three voices allow a fuller harmonic sonority than do two voices, without the registral cluttering than can occur if many voices are involved. The general "rules" of two-part counterpoint apply to three or more parts as well, with only a few exceptions.

Parallel octaves and fifths are, as always, forbidden. But *direct octaves and fifths* are usually possible in three-voice writing if one of the voices involved is in the middle, and if one of the voices involved is moving by step. Diminished 5th moving to perfect 5th, which would not be correct in two voices, is possible in three parts, if the harmony is resolving a first inversion diminished triad to a first inversion major or minor triad, such as vii°⁶-I⁶.

The classification of intervals between the parts remains the same as in two voices except for the *perfect 4th*. A perfect 4th is dissonant in two voices, but completely acceptable in three or more parts as long as the lowest voice is not involved. If there is a perfect 4th between the bass and any upper part, the harmony is heard in six-four inversion, and must receive special treatment. But if the perfect 4th is in the upper parts, it simply serves to fill in the triad and is completely correct.

In writing for three (or more) voices, all the contrapuntal textures mentioned earlier are used: For a sense of distinct voices, *different rhythmic identities*, or *different melodic contours*, or *imitation* among the parts may be used. It also frequently happens that all voices are not of equal importance or distinction. Parallel pitch or rhythmic motion may align two voices while a third voice is free, and parallelisms and patterning may be used to subordinate accompaniment parts, allowing more important parts to emerge.

Invertibility is possible in three voices. If the parts are truly invertible, any one of the three can serve as the bass. As in double counterpoint, the most likely pitfalls here are perfect 5ths that are acceptable between parts, but invert to perfect 4ths when an upper part becomes the bass line. This must be avoided unless the resulting six-four chord is plausible in terms of six-four function. Three-voice invertible counterpoint is also called **triple counterpoint**.

Example 17a shows three lines numbered 1, 2, and 3. Example 17b shows them inverted to put the middle line (2) in the bass, and example 17c shows them inverted again, this time putting the original soprano part (1) in the bass. In triple counterpoint, six different arrangements of the voices are possible, though some of these will be more pleasing than others.

In the examples below,

$\begin{smallmatrix}1\\2\\3\end{smallmatrix} \begin{smallmatrix}3\\1\\2\end{smallmatrix} \begin{smallmatrix}2\\3\\1\end{smallmatrix}$ are used, but $\begin{smallmatrix}1\\3\\2\end{smallmatrix} \begin{smallmatrix}2\\1\\3\end{smallmatrix} \begin{smallmatrix}3\\2\\1\end{smallmatrix}$ are also possible.

17a.

G:

17b.

17c.

Double and triple counterpoint are not just contrapuntal tricks. Their compositional purpose is to maintain motivic identity while allowing some variation, and to promote equality among contrapuntal voices.

FUGUE

A fugue is a work that features imitative counterpoint among a specified number of voices, and that follows a particular pattern of transposition as the voices make their first entrances. Fugues are most likely to have three, four, or five voices, but fugues have been written with as few as two and as many as six or more voices.

A fugue begins with a theme stated in the tonic key in one voice, usually unaccompanied. This theme is called the **subject**. After the theme is completed, the second voice enters, once again with the theme, now transposed to the level of the dominant, that is, up a fifth or down a fourth from the first entry. This second statement of the theme, now transposed, is called the **answer**. The answer may be an exact transposition of the subject, called a **real answer**, or it may be somewhat altered intervalically, in which case it is called a **tonal answer**. The distinction between tonal and real answers is discussed below. For the present discussion it will not matter if the answer is tonal or real.

When the second voice enters with the answer, the first voice accompanies it with counterpoint. If this same counterpoint is used to accompany subsequent statements of the subject and the answer, it is called a **countersubject**.

The third voice of the fugue enters with the subject in the tonic key again, while the second voice accompanies, possibly with the countersubject, and the first voice accompanies freely. When the third voice has completed the subject, the fourth voice enters with the answer (on the dominant again), while the third voice has the countersubject and voices one and two are free. This subject-answer, tonic-dominant alternation continues until all the voices have entered. This part of the fugue is called the **exposition**.

Exposition in four voices:

1. soprano subject countersubject free--
                             2. alto answer   countersubject free--------------------
                                         3. tenor subject countersubject
                                                     4. bass answer

Notes on the Exposition

The order of entries shown here is soprano, alto, tenor, bass, but many other orderings are possible, such as tenor, alto, soprano, bass; or tenor, bass, soprano, alto, etc. Remember also that fugues commonly have anywhere from three to five voices; the exposition will consist of subject-answer alternations until all the voices are in. Not all fugues have a consistent countersubject. Although the exposition outlined above keeps the countersubject always above the subject-answer, for practical use throughout the fugue, the countersubject is nearly always invertible (at the octave or fifteenth) with the subject-answer. The exposition in the outline shows each voice entering in direct succession, but frequently a measure or two of free counterpoint appears in the exposition, especially after the second entry. The purpose of this free material is to make a harmonic *link* between entries, adjusting the harmony to prepare for the subject in the tonic key.

Continuation of the Fugue

After all the voices have made their entries, there is likely to be a passage in free counterpoint that is derived from motives used in the exposition. This is very often a sequential passage, and frequently makes a modulation to a closely related key. A passage in a fugue in which the subject and answer are not present is called an **episode**. Episodes often concentrate on a relatively small amount of motivic material, and use double or triple invertible counterpoint for variety from one episode to the next. Generally episodes lead to new statements of the subject and answer, often in keys other than the original.

A set of entries after the first episode is often referred to as a **second exposition.** This is followed by a second episode, a third exposition, and so on. Subsequent sets of entries are rarely as systematic and complete as those in the original exposition.

In general, the ongoing form of a fugue is made up of subject-answer entries in some or all voices, alternating with episodes. The number of expositions and episodes varies enormously from fugue to fugue, and the keys of transpositions, while usually those closely related to the original key, do not follow any fixed scheme. Fugues sometimes contain complexities, such as multiple subjects, or augmentation, diminution, or inversion of the subject. Therefore a fugue is not really a form, but rather an elaborate set of contrapuntal and formal procedures that can be worked out in many different ways.

The end of the fugue frequently presents the subject over a **pedal point** (most likely a tonic pedal). Another technique often seen toward the end of the fugue is **stretto.** A stretto is a series of subjects and answers in which each voice enters before the preceding voice has completed its statement. The effect of parts piling on successively is especially effective in creating climactic tensions.

IMITATION: REAL VERSUS TONAL

In looking at fugues from the common practice period, and in earlier imitative counterpoint as well, we see that an adjustment is sometimes made in the exact intervals of an imitation at the fifth. Look at the imitation in example 18, which shows the beginning of the second (c-minor) fugue of *The Well-Tempered Clavier, Book 1* by Bach.

18.

In an exact imitation, the fourth note of the answer * would be D, not C. The C is substituted to support the sense of c minor as the tonic. The music is going to tonicize g minor as the answer continues, and this little change at the beginning of the answer simply slows that process down slightly, and helps subordinate g minor to the original key. Because the imitation is slightly changed so as to support the overall tonic, this is called **tonal imitation**. Imitation that is exact is called **real imitation**. There can be many complex considerations in choosing between real and tonal imitation, and if adjustments are to be made, one must decide which notes to change and what to change them to. For our purposes, we will consider only some general rules of thumb, and see how these apply to fugues.

The most likely place for adjustment to be made is in imitating the very beginning of the subject. The first four or five notes or the first rhythmic group of the subject are together called the **head of the subject**. As a general rule, if the head of the subject contains a strong dominant, the answer will adjust so as to reply with tonic in the corresponding place. An answer that is adjusted is called a **tonal answer**, an answer that is an exact imitation is called a **real answer**.

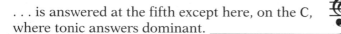

Going back to our Bach example, example 19 illustrates how the head of the subject with its strong dominant note here . . .

. . . is answered at the fifth except here, on the C, where tonic answers dominant.

Note that *after the head of the subject*, even a strong dominant, such as the one on the downbeat of measure 2, is answered in real imitation at the fifth, not with the tonic.

To summarize, in imitating the head of the subject, normally, *tonic answers dominant*, and *dominant answers tonic*. While this general rule will provide significant help in understanding tonal imitation and tonal answers in fugues, it must be recognized as a simplification of a potentially complicated topic. Sometimes a real answer is used when tonal imitation might have been expected, and sometimes the adjustments made in a tonal answer are surprising. Some fugues have modulating subjects or other built-in complications. In addition, many fugues that have tonal answers in the first exposition use both tonal and real answers as the fugues go on. The considerable variety in the use of tonal imitation makes analysis of real works especially valuable.

Below are a few more examples from *The Well-Tempered Clavier, Book 1*. These show only whether the subject has a real or tonal answer at the beginning of the fugue. In the examples of tonal answers, the point of tonal imitation is marked (*). Each fugue has many other interesting and beautiful features, and each is worthy of study as a whole work.

Example 20 shows Fugue 1, C major. Real answer—the head of the subject contains no strong dominant.

20.

Example 21 offers Fugue 16, g minor. Tonal answer—first note of the subject is the dominant. The tonal answer sacrifices the half step motive at the beginning, but strengthens the g-minor tonic.

21.

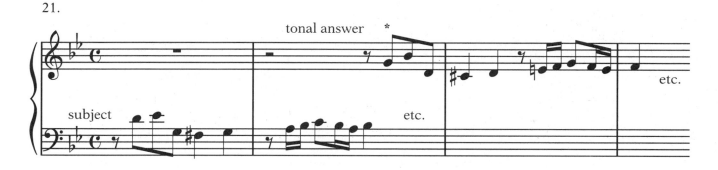

Next, we see Fugue 6, d minor (example 22). Real answer—there is no dominant at the head of the subject.

22.

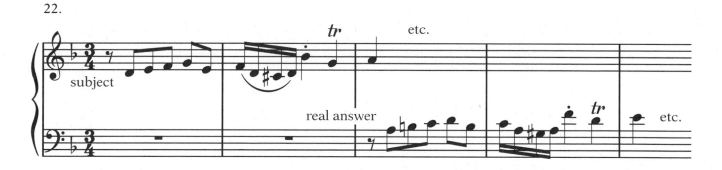

Example 23 shows Fugue 17, A-flat major. Tonal answer because of the strong E-flat (dominant) in the opening arpeggio.

23.

Finally, example 24 offers Fugue 12, f minor. Tonal answer, subject starts on the dominant. The first C (dominant) is answered with tonic, but the second is not, perhaps to preserve the intervalic character of the subject, and also for harmonic reasons.

24.

SUGGESTIONS FOR ANALYSIS AND FURTHER READING

Analysis

The keyboard music of J. S. Bach provides an excellent source for analysis of tonal counterpoint. For imitative counterpoint (but not fugue), the *Two- and Three-Part Inventions* are a good place to begin. Two-, three-, and four-voice counterpoint that is often not imitative can be found in the *French Suites* and *English Suites* and in the preludes of *The Well-Tempered Clavier*. Fugues will, of course, be found in *The Well-Tempered Clavier*, as well. Also not to be overlooked are the preludes and fugues for organ, and the chorale preludes of the *Orgelbüchlein*. Since Bach's general style is contrapuntal, nearly every instrumental and choral work provides excellent examples for tonal counterpoint.

Because the music of Bach is so rich in counterpoint and so readily available for study, one might concentrate on Bach and never discover the distinct contrapuntal styles of other Baroque composers. It is interesting, though, to compare the counterpoint of Handel, for example, to that of Bach. Corelli, Couperin, and Purcell, among others, all have distinct styles.

Finally, the study of counterpoint ought to include classical and romantic versions of contrapuntal forms (fugues of Mozart and Beethoven, for example), as well as a more general analysis of counterpoint drawn from works of the eighteenth and nineteenth centuries.

Further Reading

There are numerous texts on the subject of counterpoint, just as there are for harmony. Two books that have been widely used are *Counterpoint* by Walter Piston (W. W. Norton) and *Counterpoint* by Kent Kennan (Prentice-Hall).

PART 5

Phrasing, Structure, and a Glossary of Forms

CADENCE TYPES

A **phrase** is a musical statement that has a beginning, a middle, and an end. A piece of music usually contains many phrases, and the phrases themselves can often be divided into clear beginning, middle, and end subphrases. Analysts may disagree on matters of phrasing in the context of a given piece, especially in defining the length of a phrase as opposed to a subphrase or a group of phrases. Nevertheless, the notion of phrasing is essential to understanding common practice period music, and consistency in the definitions can be viewed as a desirable, if not always attainable goal.

The phrase ending, called the **cadence,** varies from one phrase to the next both in character and in degree of finality. We can review the several common cadence types, defined as follows.

Full or authentic cadence
V-I. Called **perfect authentic** if the tonic note is in the soprano of the I chord. Called **imperfect authentic** if $\hat{3}$ or $\hat{5}$ is in the soprano of the I chord. **Perfect authentic** is by far the most common final cadence.

Half cadence
Any cadence on V. Common approaches to V include I, ii⁶, IV, V/V, etc.

Deceptive cadence

V-vi or V-VI. Leading tone resolves to tonic! Note that not every V-vi (or VI) progression is a cadence.

deceptive

I   ii6   V - 7   vi

Plagal cadence

IV–I or iv–i. Common "amen" progression, rarely seen as a final cadence in extended concert music.

plagal

V   .   I   IV   I

Phrygian cadence

iv6–V. A type of half cadence belonging to minor keys only. Named after the Phrygian mode (which begins with a half step) because of half step in bass as iv6 steps down to V.

Phrygian

i   iv6   V

PHRASE RELATIONSHIPS

The way in which phrases relate to one another varies enormously from piece to piece and from moment to moment within a given piece. The discourse of the phrasing, that is, whether each phrase is answered, continued, interrupted, contradicted, overlapped, etc., gives every piece a unique shape. Sensitivity to phrasing is therefore essential for performance, and the study of phrasing must be a lifelong pursuit.

At the outset, we can define one phrase relationship that is very common in tonal music, the **antecedent-consequent** (sometimes called **statement-answer** or **question-answer**) relationship. In this model, a musical statement that is somehow incomplete is answered and balanced by another statement that supplies **closure.** In the classical style, antecedent-consequent phrases occur frequently in two-, four-, or eight-measure units.

A typical pattern might be a four-measure phrase (or half phrase) ending with a half cadence, answered by a similar four-measure phrase ending with a full cadence.

THE MAGIC FLUTE

Mozart

four measures to a half cadence

answered by four measures to a full cadence

etc.

Not all phrases form antecedent-consequent relationships. It frequently happens that two or more antecedent phrases may be answered by a single consequent. When any number of phrases are linked together, either an antecedent pair or a larger number of phrases, this multi-phrase unit is called a **period.** The end of the period achieves some degree of closure for all of its component phrases. The entire example above constitutes one period.

SEQUENCE

Often the musical context calls for pushing forward, not rounding and balancing. The next example, from Mozart's familiar C-major Sonata, K. 545, shows a **sequence** in measures 5–9. A sequence is a pattern or fragment that is transposed and repeated, often several times in succession. Because of the repetition of material, the musical effect of a sequence often has more to do with its transpositions (the sense that it is moving somewhere) than with the material itself. In this case, the pattern emphasizes a stepwise descent that occurs on the downbeat of each measure. If this sequence were completely balanced with the first phrase, the pattern might be leading to the tonic chord in measure 8; but since the sequence doesn't stop, but rather pushes on into measure 9, and since measure 9 pushes the scales further, ultimately leading through V/V to V in measures 11–12, we see that the whole sequence is part of a transition that increases emphasis on the dominant. The two phrases that begin this piece, measures 1–4 and measures 5–12, are not balanced in terms of length and do not have an antecedent-consequent relationship to one another. The sequence has the effect of stretching out the phrase here as the piece also opens up harmonically and registrally.

SONATA K. 545

Mozart

Sometimes a sequence helps to spur a transition, as in the example above, and sometimes the sequence itself modulates, creating a new tonicization with every repetition of the pattern. The next example, from the d-minor fugue from *The Well-Tempered Clavier, Book 1,* by J. S. Bach, shows such a pattern, which is called a **modulating sequence.**

In this case, the root harmonies are moving by fifth, as labeled in the example. Since the first two members of the sequence are V/iv–iv and V/III–III, one might wonder why the next part of the sequence is VI–ii°, rather than V/ii°–ii°. The reason is simple: ii° in minor is a diminished triad, and therefore has no dominant. B-flat (VI) is V of E-flat, which is not a closely related key to d-minor.

FUGUE IN D MINOR
WELL-TEMPERED CLAVIER, BOOK 1

J. S. Bach

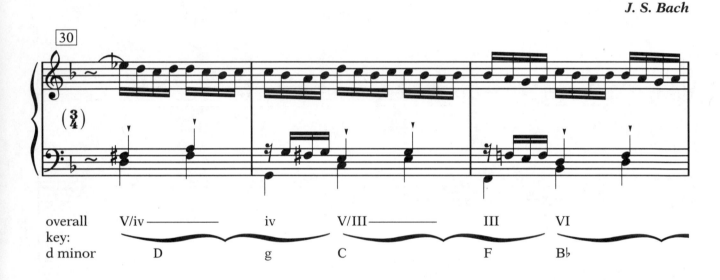

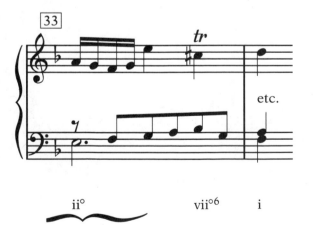

Many musical variants can affect our sense of the finality of cadences and the balance of phrases. Some effects to watch for in analysis include **cadential extension** (in which the end portion of the phrase is elongated, usually through repetition of the cadence), and **overlap** (in which the cadence of one phrase coincides exactly with the beginning of the next phrase). **Contrapuntal texture,** in which different contrapuntal voices do not necessarily arrive at cadence points simultaneously, can also complicate our perception of phrasing.

STRUCTURAL LINE

As important as cadence and phrase relationships are to musical coherence, so also are two other factors, namely **long-range voice leading** and **overall harmonic progression.** Large-scale harmonic structure was briefly discussed in Part 3; the example below will serve to illustrate both melodic and harmonic structure over the course of an antecedent-consequent phrase.

SONATA K. 333
3RD MOVEMENT

Mozart

Here is an antecedent-consequent pair of phrase halves that together form a balanced, eight-measure phrase. To understand the long-range voice leading here, we must break down the melodic phrase into its smallest logical subgroups, each a unit of two measures (referred to here as *groups*). Melodically, the first group presents two arpeggios, first tonic, then a stepwise expansion to E-flat, G, and A, all part of a dominant 9th chord. The second group (measures 3–4) does not answer the leading tone A that ended the first group, but it fills in the arpeggios, coming down the scale from the high F, through the appoggiatura D on the downbeat of measure 4, getting as far as C on the third beat. In terms of generalized voice leading, we can see that, in the first four measures, there has been a stepwise descent, F to E-flat to D to C, or $\hat{5}$-$\hat{4}$-$\hat{3}$-$\hat{2}$. We can also see that each of these two measure groups points specifically to B-flat for resolution, and that the B-flat they point to is registrally specific—it must be the one above middle C. Harmonically, the first phrase (first two groups together) is easy to summarize: It moves from I to V.

Melodically, the third group is very similar to the first, except that it now fills in the space between F and B-flat. Why don't the B-flats in measure 5 satisfy the need for this note, as set up by the first two groups? Because these B-flats occur in the middle of this group. The B-flat that will answer the end of the first group (A), and the end of the second group (C), must also be an end point. The third group ends in measure 6, once again leaving off on the leading tone. In the final group (measures 7–8), the A and C are brought together melodically, and both literally resolve to B-flat on the downbeat. Thus the $\hat{5}$-$\hat{4}$-$\hat{3}$-$\hat{2}$ descent that occurs in the first two groups is completed here, and the leading tone is also resolved. Harmonically the second phrase (third and fourth groups) answers the first, moving I-V-I.

An outline like the one below summarizes this melodic and harmonic motion.

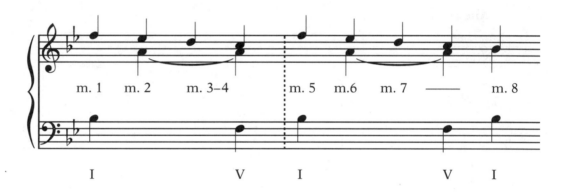

A long-range stepwise structure like the one seen here is sometimes called a **structural line.** The musician who first pointed out the tremendous analytical significance of the structural line was the theorist **Heinrich Schenker** (1868–1935). Schenker developed a graphic method of musical analysis, in which details of a composition could be gradually subordinated to the work's larger melodic and harmonic motions, until finally the ultimate background structure was revealed. For Schenker, the background structure consisted of the structural line and the underlying harmonic framework. His life's work was devoted to demonstrating that coherent pieces of tonal music share a basic architecture: Over entire movements, most works have a structural line that descends toward the tonic from the third ($\hat{3}$-$\hat{2}$-$\hat{1}$) or from the fifth ($\hat{5}$-$\hat{4}$-$\hat{3}$-$\hat{2}$-$\hat{1}$); this structural line is usually supported by an underlying I-V-I harmonic structure. Schenker's method of reductive analysis is used not only to lay bare this basic architecture, but also to show how the various compositional levels in a piece relate to make a uniquely detailed whole.

Schenker's analytic method is quite complex, and lies well outside the scope of this book (interested students should consult the bibliography at the end of this part for some source materials on Schenkerian analysis). But it is possible to gain many analytical insights from the general idea that music makes clear stepwise patterns supported by a fundamental harmonic structure over the length of a period and over the length of an entire movement. It is worthwhile to attempt to trace the large scale patterns of music, and to become sensitive to longer-range connections.

FORM

The idea of musical forms in the eighteenth and nineteenth centuries may conjure up a picture of composers working from preset plans of themes, modulations, etc. It is important to understand that this was almost never the case; in fact, many of our ideas about specific forms have developed in periods after these forms were commonly written. Therefore, the forms that will be described here should not be regarded as sets of rules that were followed by composers of the common practice period. Rather, they should be viewed as typical formal outlines based on observation of many, many pieces. There is actually a tremendous variety not only in the broad formal outlines of individual pieces, but also in the way that thematic material, gesture, length, register, dynamics, etc. interact to produce formal moments.

The forms described below are some of those more commonly encountered in theory courses. There are many other specific forms, and many possible variants of formal ideas described only briefly here. Specific formal terms may be looked up in *The New Grove Dictionary of Music and Musicians, The Harvard Dictionary of Music,* etc.

Baroque Forms, Genres, and Terms

Aria: Not really a specific form, an aria is a song in an opera, cantata, or oratorio. It is often elaborate in musical design and vocal effects, and tends to express feelings rather than to advance the plot, since comprehensibility of words is not necessarily a high priority. Also see *da capo aria* and *recitative.*

Bar form: A German song form dating back to medieval times, following the scheme *a a b* (*Stollen, Stollen, Abgesang*). Often the form of chorale tunes harmonized by Bach and others.

Binary form: Division of a piece into two parts, each part normally repeated (‖:a:‖:b:‖). Also called *simple binary*—compare to *rounded binary* of the Classical period. The Baroque binary form is found in suite movements (allemande, courante, sarabande, gigue, etc.) as well as other instrumental pieces. In major, the "a" section most often moves from I to V, though it is possible for it to remain in I. In minor, the most common "a" section move is from i to III, but the minor v and the tonic are also possible goals of the "a" section. The "b" section returns to the tonic to close the form (if the "a" section didn't modulate, the "b" section will usually move away from the tonic and then come back). Also see *ternary form.*

Cantata: A work for chorus, soloists, and instrumental ensemble on a sacred or secular theme. The size of the performing ensemble is highly variable. The text is usually metaphorical or contemplative, as opposed to narrative. Cantatas may contain choral movements, solo arias, duets, and recitatives.

Chorale: Not a specific form, a chorale is a hymn tune of the German Protestant church. Chorale singing was an important feature of the German Protestant (Lutheran) movement from its beginnings in the sixteenth century. Chorale tunes harmonized by Bach (and others) came from many sources, and in many cases predate Bach by 200 years or more. Most of the tunes are modal (rather than tonal) in their origins, and may sound tonally unsettled to the modern ear. Bach and others used these familiar tunes as a basis for cantatas, oratorios, and passions, as well as for elaborate keyboard versions called *organ chorales* or *chorale preludes*.

Chorale prelude: A work for organ that uses a chorale either in elaborated or simple form (stated in long notes) surrounded by elaborate polyphony. More generally this term describes any work having this texture, especially many choral movements of cantatas.

Concerto: A work that contrasts a soloist or a group of soloists against a larger orchestra. If the work is for a group of soloists it is a *concerto grosso.* The group of soloists is called the *concertino* while the larger ensemble is called the *ripieno* (or *tutti*). In late Baroque concerti, the first movement form is based on an opening tutti statement called the *ritornello,* which returns from time to time (sometimes fragmented or transposed) contrasted with the soloists' more varied material.

Continuo: Not a form, but a compositional element during the Baroque, the continuo consists of two players providing the harmonic outline of a piece. A bass instrument (bass, 'cello, bassoon) plays the bass line while a chord-playing instrument (harpsichord, organ, lute) plays the bass and the essential harmonic progression. Virtually all Baroque compositions involving more than two instrumentalists employ continuo.

Da capo aria: A song form typical of Baroque operas, oratorios, and cantatas, following the a b a form (ternary form). The "a" section is closed on the tonic, while the "b" section provides harmonic contrast. After the completion of the "b" section, the performers turn back to the beginning (*da capo*) and repeat the "a" section. The close of the "a" section (and therefore the end of the movement) is a full cadence, often marked with a fermata. Also see *ternary form.*

Fugue: Not a form, but, in instrumental and especially keyboard works, a contrapuntal procedure in which a theme (*subject*) is introduced successively in all parts (most often, 3, 4, or 5 voices). The introduction of the subject follows a specific pattern of transposition (first tonic, then dominant, then tonic, etc.) until all voices are in. The transposition of the subject to the dominant is called the *answer.* The answer is called a *real answer* if it is a literal transposition of the subject to the pitch level of the dominant. If the answer has undergone some intervalic adjustment as well as transposition, it is called a *tonal answer.* The subject may be accompanied by a consistent counterpoint called the *countersubject*. Successive statements of the subject and answer follow each other without overlap. A set of overlapping statements is called a *stretto*. Sections of the fugue where the subject/answer are not present are called *episodes*. See Part 4 for a more complete discussion of fugue.

Ground bass: A repeating bass pattern that underlies an entire composition, creating a kind of variations. Pieces using the ground bass idea include the English *ground*, the *passacaglia*, and the *chaconne*. In a passacaglia, the repeating figure sometimes appears in the upper parts; in a chaconne, the basis for the composition is a repeating harmonic progression, so that the bass line itself may be variable. Use of a ground is often associated with the idea of lamentation.

Mass: A work that may call for chorus, soloists, and orchestra, in which the text is the specific liturgical Latin mass of the Roman Catholic Church. By the late Baroque period, a mass might include all the musical variety found in operas and cantatas, including recitatives, arias, duets, and choral movements.

Opera: A staged drama for chorus, soloists, and orchestra, typically including recitatives, arias, duets, choral movements, and instrumental movements.

Oratorio: An unstaged drama on a sacred or secular subject for chorus, soloists, and orchestra. Includes all the musical types normally found in operas and cantatas. Unlike most cantatas, the text is a narrative (as opposed to a reflection on a theme). It is like an opera, but written for concert performance rather than the theater.

Recitative: A vocal piece that serves as declamation of text in opera, oratorio, cantata, etc. Unlike an aria, a recitative is not usually songlike, in that it features syllabic declamation on repeated notes, irregular rhythm, and simple, nonmotivic chordal accompaniment. Frequently precedes an aria, supplying the background story on which the aria may then reflect.

Sonata: The term sonata means sounded (i.e., played on an instrument) as opposed to sung. In the Baroque, solo, duo, and trio sonatas are common, and follow a variety of formal schemes. Note that the term *sonata form* does not apply to Baroque sonatas—sonata form is a development of the Classical period. See also *trio sonata*.

Suite: A set of stylized dances for solo, chamber, or orchestral forces. A typical suite includes an *allemande, courante, sarabande,* and *gigue,* as well as other possibilities, including *minuet, air, passepied, polonaise, bourrée, gavotte,* etc. All movements are in the same key and show binary form. *Allemande*—moderate tempo, duple time; *courante*—somewhat faster, triple time, often with hemiolas; *sarabande*—slow triple time, often stressing the second beat; *gigue*—quick tempo, compound duple meter, often including fugal imitations, most likely to be the last movement.

Ternary form: A three-part form that can be summarized as a b a. Typically, each section is closed harmonically by a full cadence. Baroque instrumental pieces in ternary form include paired dance movements, such as minuet-trio-minuet. In this model, the "b" section contrasts with "a" in terms of material, and makes a complete close before the return of "a." Also in ternary form is the *da capo aria*; here the form is more continuous, and "b" section, while closed harmomically, may not be highly contrasted with "a."

Trio sonata: The characteristic chamber music combination of the Baroque, a *trio sonata is usually scored for four players*. The combination consists of two single-line upper-part instruments (such as two violins, or two flutes, or flute & violin, etc.) and continuo (a bass line instrument plus a chord-playing instrument). Typical formal plans call for a four-movement work (slow-fast-slow-fast) sometimes called a *sonata da chiesa*; or a multi-movement suite sometimes called a *sonata da camera*.

Classical Forms, Genres, and Terms

Alberti bass: A type of accompaniment figure popular in the Classical period, an Alberti bass is an accompaniment pattern made up of broken chords played in steady rhythm. An example can be seen in Mozart's Sonata in C major, K. 545, on page 91.

Binary form (rounded binary): Developed from the binary form of the Baroque, this form divides a piece into two repeated sections. *Rounding* occurs when, at the conclusion of the second section, a strong thematic reference is made to the opening of the movement. Thus, the scheme ‖:a:‖:b a':‖. The harmonic outline of the form is identical to that of the Baroque binary; the rounding coincides with the return to the tonic key.

Minuet and trio: Stylized dance movements originating in the Baroque, characteristically in 3/4 time, the Classical minuet-trio-minuet are a pair of rounded binary forms commonly seen as the second or third movement of a four-movement work. The form can be outlined as follows:

	minuet	trio	minuet
	‖: a :‖: b a' :‖	‖: c :‖: d c' :‖	‖ a ‖ b a' ‖
typical harmonic scheme: (all variants listed under Baroque binary are possible)	I-V --- I	I-V --- I the key of the trio may be that of the minuet (with or without a mode change) or a related key	I-V --- I

Note the following points: In terms of formal type, the minuet and the trio are identical. Each is a fully independent rounded binary form with its own thematic material. While a few trios are followed by a short harmonic transition back to the key of the minuet, this is relatively rare. Usually the minuet simply returns after the trio.

The formal plan for the minuet-trio movement can be summarized as A B A, (A = minuet and B = trio). This is a *three-part or ternary form*. Note the difference between this overall form and the internal form of the minuet or trio. In the overall ternary form, the "B" section (the whole trio) is entirely independent of the "A" section; the trio is a separate little piece that has a complete ending of its own. In contrast, the "b" section of a rounded binary form is harmonically incomplete, and requires the "a'" section to make its ending.

Rondo form: A form often used for last movements, with characteristically sprightly themes. The simple rondo consists of an alternation between its opening theme "a," and other, contrasting material, for example: a b a c a d a etc. The "a" theme always appears in the tonic, while the other material modulates to related keys and then makes transitions back to prepare for each return of "a." Also see *sonata rondo.*

Scherzo: Developed from the Classical minuet-trio-minuet movement, the scherzo-trio-scherzo movement is identical in form (or may be somewhat expanded), and is frequently found as the third movement in multi-movement works of Beethoven and later composers. It has 3/4 meter, rapid tempo, and often a driving and accented or abrupt and surprising rhythmic quality.

Sonata concerto: First movements of Classical concerti combine the sonata idea with the concerto form from the Baroque period (including the opposition of tutti and solo and the idea of the tutti ritornello in the tonic). The form includes a so-called *double exposition,* in which first the tutti play *an entire exposition without changing keys,* and then the soloist enters and begins a second exposition that follows a usual sonata outline in terms of both keys and themes. While the soloist usually begins the second exposition, the tutti generally join in quickly and the rest of the movement is shared between tutti and solo. Closing themes, development, and recapitulation follow more or less the sonata pattern. Just before the final closing material, as the orchestra arrives on a I$_4^6$ chord, the soloist inserts the *cadenza,* a free form, sometimes improvised showcase of technical and interpretive effects. As the cadenza ends, the orchestra resolves I$_4^6$ to V, and from there goes to the final tonic closing material to end the movement.

Sonata form: In Classical and Romantic instrumental music, the formal plan of many first and last movements (*sonata allegro*), as well as slow movements. A grand expansion of the rounded binary form, in sonatas "a" = exposition, "b" = development, "a'"= recapitulation. The form can be further broken down as follows:

Exposition (="a")

Development (="b")

1st theme group	*bridge*	*2nd theme group*	*closing* ‖	thematic	*retransition*
I (or i)	transition usually leading to V/V (or V/III) (half cadence)	V (or III) (sounds like new tonic)	V (or III)‖	development & harmonic instability leads to reinterpretation of V as functioning dominant	V (dominant function)

Recapitulation (="a'")

1st theme group	*bridge*	*2nd theme group*	*closing* ‖
I (or i)	reworked transition altered so as to end on half cadence in tonic key	I (or i)	I (or i)

As can be seen in the diagram above, sonata form consists of an *exposition* in which two contrasting keys are articulated by two contrasting themes or theme groups. The exposition closes in the second key, which by that time has received a great deal of confirmation as the new tonic. The *development* section is highly variable from piece to piece, sometimes using fragments of some or all of the exposition's themes, sometimes introducing new material. Harmonically, the job of the development section is to realign the harmonic relationships so that the original key can emerge as the overall tonic, and the second key is subordinated. The retransition, if present, provides dominant preparation for the recapitulation. It usually also has a somewhat thinned texture, preparing for the accent of recapitulation. The *recapitulation* restates all the material from the exposition, but with no change of key. The bridge from the exposition must be altered so as not to modulate, and often seems harmonically more complicated in the recapitulation than in the exposition.

Here are some common variants to the "basic" sonata form:

- In Classical works the *exposition is usually repeated.* This repetition becomes less common toward the nineteenth century, and eventually disappears as part of the form.

- Frequently a *slow introduction* precedes the exposition. The introduction provides dominant preparation. It is not brought back in the recap, but may figure in the development or in a coda.
- A *coda* is sometimes found after the recapitulation. The coda adds additional weight to the ending, and appears only after all the expected material from the exposition has returned.
- Sometimes, especially in Haydn, the *same theme is used for both the first and second key* in the exposition.
- Sometimes the *recap reverses the order of themes* from the exposition.
- For themes in minor keys, sometimes the *recap is in the major mode.*
- *In slow movements,* the second theme group often serves as closing too. The development section may be quite short.
- *In sonatinas,* the development section is usually greatly abbreviated or missing entirely.

Sonata rondo: A combination of sonata and rondo ideas, the sonata rondo (also called *seven-part rondo*) is diagrammed below. Frequently used for last movements.

section:	a	b	a	c	a	b	a
key:	I	V	I	quasi-development, ending on V	I	I	I

Note the difference between this form and sonata form: In sonata-rondo, there is a return of the tonic with the opening theme in the middle of the piece; in sonata form, the tonic return with the opening theme occurs only in the recapitulation. Note also the difference between sonata-rondo and simple rondo: In sonata-rondo, the "b" section is presented first in the dominant, then recapitulated later in the tonic; in simple rondo, the "b" section is not recapitulated.

Ternary form: A three-part division of a movement (as opposed to *binary form*). There is potential confusion between ternary form (A B A) and rounded binary (a | b a'). Note that in ternary form, each section is completely self-enclosed, usually with its own material and its own full cadence ending. In a rounded binary, the "a" section may be self-enclosed (it may end on I), but the "b" section never is—it ends with a half cadence or a transition back to I, and therefore requires the "a'" section for completion. The minuet–trio–minuet movement is an example of ternary form, but each constituent section, that is, the minuet alone or the trio alone, is a rounded binary.

Romantic Period Forms and Terms

Character piece: Short work, most often for piano, that expresses a particular mood, emotion, or scene. Includes many romantic period titles, such as bagatelle, impromptu, intermezzo, nocturne, caprice, etc. Form is usually either ternary or rounded binary.

Program music: Music in which the form and material are based on a story or scenario, as opposed to *absolute music,* that is, music which refers only to its own musical workings. Many large works of the nineteenth century are based on some sort of program. The terms *tone poem* and *symphonic poem* are frequently used to designate program music. Since the music is based on an extramusical program, a work in this category does not have a predictable form.

SUGGESTIONS FOR ANALYSIS AND FURTHER READING

The following books on phrasing, analysis, and form will lead interested students in a number of analytic directions, all current and useful. These are not, for the most part, textbooks, and many assume a fairly sophisticated understanding of tonal music.

General analysis and phrasing

Charles Rosen, *The Classical Style: Haydn, Mozart, Beethoven* (Viking Press)
William Rothstein, *Phrase Rhythm in Tonal Music* (Schirmer Books–Macmillan)
Donald Francis Tovey, *Essays in Musical Analysis* (Oxford University Press)

Long-range voice leading

Felix Salzer, *Structural Hearing* (Dover)
Felix Salzer and Carl Schachter, *Counterpoint in Composition* (McGraw-Hill)
Heinrich Schenker, *Der freie Satz* (in English, *Free Composition*) (Longman)
Heinrich Schenker, *Five Graphic Analyses* (Dover)

Form

For general reference to terms, as well as detailed discussion and bibliography on major topics, see *The New Grove Dictionary of Music and Musicians* (Macmillan).
Also of interest:
Douglass Green, *Form in Tonal Music* (Holt, Rinehart and Winston)
Charles Rosen, *Sonata Forms* (W. W. Norton)

PART 6

Instrumentation: Names, Ranges, Transposition

The instruments listed in this part are those most commonly used in the eighteenth- and nineteenth-century orchestra. They are listed in score order, with the names given first in English, then, in parentheses, in Italian, German, and French. The ranges specified are *written ranges for each instrument*. If the instrument transposes, it will be necessary to transpose the range given in order to know the range in actual sounds.

How to Transpose

The transposing instruments fall into two categories: those which transpose at the octave in order to avoid many, many ledger lines in notation (piccolo, contrabassoon, string bass), and those which exist in a number of different sizes (clarinet, horn, trumpet) or are auxiliary instruments (English horn). For these, the player generally learns only one set of basic fingerings, which can be used on all the instruments in the same family. Thus a written C has a particular fingering on the clarinet, but since there are clarinets of many different sizes, that C fingering produces different pitches depending upon the size of the instrument played.

For practical purposes, transpositions are quite easily calculated. If an instrument is said to be "in" a particular pitch (clarinet in B♭, for example), that means that a written C produces the pitch specified in the name. In other words, for the B♭ clarinet, when the player fingers a C, the resulting pitch is B♭. Therefore, the sounding pitch is a whole step lower than the written pitch. For clarinet in A, the written C produces a sounding A. Therefore, the sounding pitch is a minor 3rd lower than written. For horn in F, the written C is a sounding F. Therefore, the sounding pitch is a perfect 5th below written. For English horn, the transposition is not part of the name. One must simply know that the English horn is pitched in F (i.e., it sounds a perfect 5th below written).

Special Factors in Notation for French Horn

In scores from the Classical period, the French horn is called for in many different keys (generally the key of the piece). This is because, before the invention of valves, the horn was limited to the pitches in the overtone series according to the length of the instrument. For every different key, the player inserted a "crook" of a particular length to adjust the length of the horn. Therefore we see horn in E♭, horn in A, etc. For all these transpositions, simply follow the rule given above (written C is a sounding E♭, written C is a sounding A, etc.), always transposing *down*.

After the invention of valves, horn in F became the notational standard. In the treble clef, read horns down a perfect 5th. For horn notated in the bass clef, in some older scores it is necessary to read up a perfect 4th, rather than down a perfect 5th, although this notation is no longer used.

For contemporary scores, bear in mind that many scores are "in C," meaning that all instruments are notated as they will actually sound. In this case the parts will provide the transpositions for the players. Look for a note at the beginning of the score to indicate whether the score is transposed or not.

Not every instrument is listed on the chart. Students needing more information may consult any orchestration book. *The Study of Orchestration* (2nd ed.) by Samuel Adler (Norton) is excellent.

Woodwinds

Instrument (Italian, German, French)	Range & Clefs as written—transpose if necessary	Transposing?	How?
Piccolo (ottavino, Kleine Flote, petite flute)	*8va*	yes	sounds an octave above written
Flute (flauto, Flote, flute)	*8va*	no	
Oboe (oboe, Hoboe, hautbois)		no	
English Horn (corno inglese, Englisch Horn, cor anglais)		yes	sounds a perfect 5th lower than written

Woodwinds

Instrument (Italian, German, French)	Range & Clefs as written—transpose if necessary	Transposing?	How?
Clarinet (clarinetto, Klarinette, clarinette)		yes	B♭ clarinet sounds a whole step lower than written. A clarinet sounds a minor 3rd below written. B♭ bass clarinet sounds a major 9th down if written in treble clef, a major 2nd down in bass clef. Piccolo clarinet (E♭) sounds a minor 3rd higher than written.
Saxophone (sassofone, Saxophon, saxophone)		yes	B♭ soprano sounds a major 2nd below written E♭ alto sounds a major 6th below written B♭ tenor sounds a major 9th below written E♭ baritone sounds an octave + major 6th below written
Bassoon (fagotto, Fagott, basson)		no	
Contrabassoon (contrafagotto, Kontrafagot, contrebasson)		yes	sounds an octave below written

continued

Brass and Timpani

Instrument (Italian, German, French)	Range & Clefs as written—transpose if necessary	Transposing?	How?
Horn (corno, Horn, cor)		yes	in Classical period as specified in score. From mid-nineteenth century horn parts are usually in F—sounds a perfect 5th lower than written, though, in older scores, if notated in bass clef, horns *may* sound a perfect 4th above written.
Trumpet (tromba, Trompete, trompette)		maybe	trumpet in C sounds as written; trumpet in B♭ sounds a major 2nd below written.
Trombone (trombone, Posaune, trombone) (range for tenor trombone)		no	
Tuba (tuba, Tuba, tuba)	*8va bassa*	no	
Timpani (timpane, Pauken, timbales)		no	the range given here is the pre-twentieth-century range. Throughout the Classical and Romantic periods, timpani were tuned by hand, with one tuning per drum per movement. The tunings are usually specified at the left side of the first page of score, where the timpani are listed among the instruments. Modern timpani are tuned with a pedal mechanism that can be changed very quickly and can also produce glissando effects. While works of the Classical and early Romantic period generally call for two drums, later scores often call for three or four drums of different sizes. With a set of four modern pedal drums the range expands to

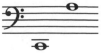

Strings

Instrument (Italian, German, French)	Range & Clefs as written—transpose if necessary	Transposing?	How?
Violin (violino, Violine or Geige, violon)		no	Note: orchestral writing virtually never goes this high.
Viola (viola, Bratsche, alto)		no	
'Cello (violoncello Violoncelle, violoncelle)		no	Note: cello also uses the tenor clef.
String Bass or Double Bass (contrabasso, Kontrabass, contre basse)		yes	sounds an octave below written. Note also a complication in the range: Some basses have a low C extension, some go only to low E. Bass also uses tenor clef.

Overtone Series

A musical tone is a blend of the **fundamental** (the lowest part of the tone) and simultaneously sounding **overtones** (also called **harmonics** or **partials**). The relationship of the fundamental to the overtones is a consistent physical property called the **overtone series** (below). All wind, brass, and stringed instruments, and voices as well, produce tones blended of fundamental and overtone sounds, all along the overtone series. The relative strength or weakness of particular overtones accounts for differences in timbre. The fundamental is often the main pitch we hear, because it is louder than the overtones in the blend. But many instrumental techniques isolate overtones so that these are the main sounds heard. In wind instruments, the fundamental notes are those produced by an air column vibrating along the full length of the instrument's tube. The tube's basic length can be adjusted by means of opening or closing holes, but the fundamental range is quite limited. Blowing harder (overblowing) causes shorter vibrations to dominate the sound. Overtones make up all the higher pitches on wind instruments. In the same way, brass instruments use overtones for most of their range. In the strings, special playing techniques bring out particular overtones, which are valued for their unique silvery timbre. Composers often make decisions about instrumental doublings in order to reinforce particular overtones.

Great C is the fundamental, and is also the first partial and first harmonic. Small c is the second partial or second harmonic, but is usually called the first overtone. Small g is the third partial or harmonic, and the second overtone (and so on). The intervals of the series over the fundamental are the same for any fundamental pitch. The partials with black noteheads are only approximately notated, since they sound somewhat lower than any conventional tuning system can show.

SUGGESTIONS FOR FURTHER READING

An all-around excellent recent text on orchestration is Samuel Adler, *The Study of Orchestration* (W. W. Norton). Another interesting book, more of a study of orchestral practice than an orchestration text, is Norman Del Mar, *Anatomy of the Orchestra* (University of California Press). Three classic texts on the topic are Hector Berlioz, *Treatise on Instrumentation*, translated by Theodore Front (Kalmus), Cecil Forsyth, *Orchestration* (MacMillan), and N. Rimsky-Korsakov, *Principles of Orchestration*, translated by Edward Agate (Dover).

PART 7

Keyboard Exercises

The purpose of the following keyboard exercises is to improve the ability to imagine the sound of musical and harmonic materials. There is little point in learning scale patterns if one cannot imagine the sound of a scale, or in learning voice-leading patterns if one cannot imagine the sound of a chord progression. The ideal is to create a continuous link between what is known in the abstract, what can be heard and recognized, what can be played, and what can be imagined.

While keyboard exercises are usually a little easier for pianists than for others, the point of the exercises is not in developing piano technique, and no great pianism is required. What *is* required is regular practicing. A few minutes every day are generally sufficient for achieving the goals of the keyboard exercises.

In practicing these exercises, aim to engage not only the fingers, but also the ear and the conscious mind. Don't rely on purely physical means, such as finger patterns and positions, to memorize the progression. While consistent fingerings can certainly help facilitate smooth performance, fingerings often feel different when the exercises are transposed, and then the student may become completely lost. It is important to think as you play, to keep track of the different pitches that make up each key, to hear the melodies of both inner and outer voices in chord progressions, to imagine the whole scale or progression as one large entity.

1. *Scales* Play one-octave scales, ascending and descending, in all keys, major and harmonic minor. Don't be overly concerned with fingerings, but try to maintain a steady pace, and think about the pattern of whole and half steps, or about the key signature and exact pitch content of each key. Test yourself—play each of the following scales: D major / f minor / b minor / G major / E major / c minor / A-flat major / d minor / f-sharp minor; now try B-flat major/ c-sharp minor / D-flat major / A major / e-flat minor / F major / g minor / e minor / B major.

2. *Intervals* Pick a starting note, and from that note play each of the following intervals. Pick a different starting note each time you practice. Also practice singing the intervals: perfect 5th up; minor 3rd down; minor 6th up; diminished 5th down; major 3rd up; perfect 5th down; perfect 4th up; minor 7th down; minor 2nd up; major 6th down; major 6th up; major 3rd down; perfect 8ve up; augmented 4th down; augmented 4th up; major 7th up; perfect 4th down; minor 3rd up; major 7th down; minor 7th up.

3. *Triads* Play major, minor, diminished, or augmented triads from any given note (root). Test yourself—play each of the following triads: E major; d minor; f-sharp diminished; B-flat augmented; A-flat major;

d diminished; f minor; a minor; D-flat major; E augmented; g diminished; e-flat minor; B major; c-sharp minor, etc.

4. *Triads* Choose a key and play each of the following triads (in root position): Major keys: iii; vi; ii; V; I; vii; IV; minor keys: VI; iv; i; V; III; ii; vii.

Chord Progressions

Practice each progression in all major and minor keys unless otherwise indicated. The progressions are set up to be played most easily with three notes in the right hand and one in the left. Begin by playing the bass line alone. Sing each upper part against the bass. When transposing, think in terms of the key you are playing in, with its particular accidentals. Don't memorize fingerings only, as this method is musically unrewarding and potentially confusing.

5.

C: I V I   c: i V i

6.

G: I IV V I   g: i iv V i

7. Major keys only

F: I V vi iii IV ii V I

8. Major and minor keys. Three positions of same progression

d: i VI iv V i   i VI iv V i   i VI iv V i

Major and minor keys!

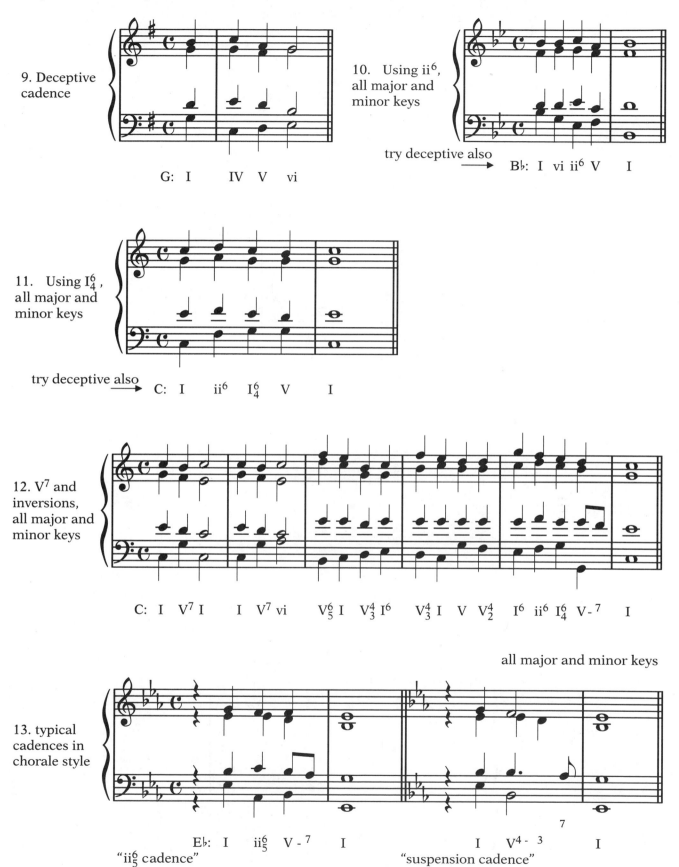

9. Deceptive cadence

G: I   IV   V   vi

10. Using ii⁶, all major and minor keys

try deceptive also → B♭: I vi ii⁶ V   I

11. Using I⁶₄ , all major and minor keys

try deceptive also → C: I   ii⁶ I⁶₄   V   I

12. V⁷ and inversions, all major and minor keys

C: I V⁷ I   I V⁷ vi   V⁶₅ I V⁴₃ I⁶   V⁴₃ I V V⁴₂   I⁶ ii⁶ I⁶₄ V-⁷   I

all major and minor keys

13. typical cadences in chorale style

E♭: I   ii⁶₅ V -⁷   I   I V⁴ - ³   I

"ii⁶₅ cadence"   "suspension cadence"

14. vii°6 chord
Phrygian cadence

minor keys only

e: i vii°6 i6 vii°6 i iv6 V

15. V/V

major and minor keys

F: I vi V6/5/V V - 4/2 I6 IV V4-3 7 I

16. vii°7, vii°7/V

major and minor keys

a: i vii°6/5 i6 vii°7 i vii°7/V V4-3 7 i

17. secondary dominants
and diminished,
passing 6/4,
major keys only

F: I V4/2/IV IV6 I6/4 vii°6/V V/V V4-3 4/2 I6 V6/5/ii ii I6 ii6/5 V-7 I

18. tonicization of V,
major keys only

C: I   IV   I⁶   vi   ii⁶₅ V-⁷ I   I   vi

G: ii   V⁶   I   ii⁶₅ V-⁷ I

19. tonicization of III,
minor keys only

d: i   V   i⁶   iv   i⁶₄   V   i   i   VI

F: IV   I⁶   vi   ii⁶₅ V-⁷ I

20. Neapolitan 6th,
major and minor keys

G: I   I⁶   N⁶   V-⁷   I

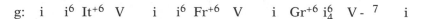

21. Augmented 6th,
major and minor keys

g: i   i⁶   It⁺⁶ V   i   i⁶   Fr⁺⁶ V   i   Gr⁺⁶ i⁶₄ V- ⁷   i

22. Neopolitan 6th,
+6 combination
with variations,
major and minor keys

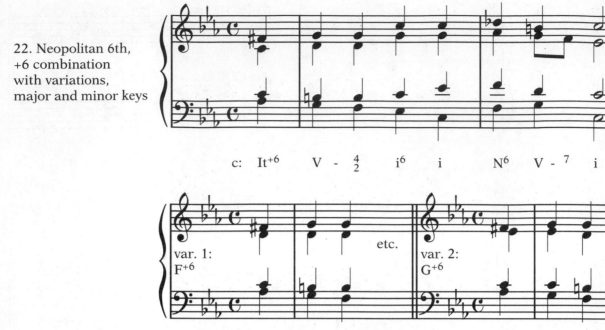

c: It⁺⁶   V - ⁴₂   i⁶   i   N⁶   V - ⁷   i

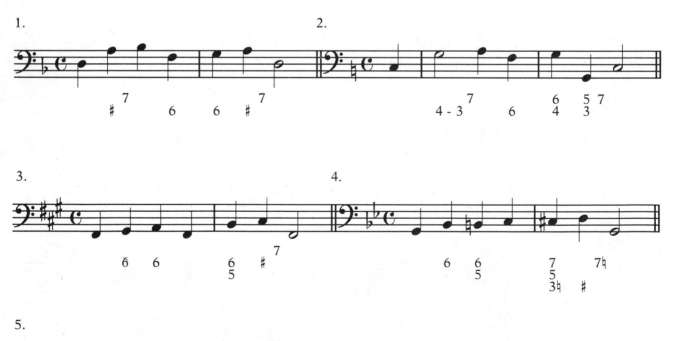

var. 1:
F⁺⁶   etc.

var. 2:
G⁺⁶   etc.

c: Fr⁺⁶   V - ⁴₂   etc.   c: Gr⁺⁶   i⁶₄   V⁴₂   etc.

Keyboard Figured Bass

1.

2.

3.

4.

5.

6.

7.

PART 8

Exercises for Parts 1–4

The exercises in this section are meant to reinforce those parts of the text for which short, straightforward examples are most helpful and appropriate. Thus there are many exercises on the musical facts contained in Part 1, such as key signatures and intervals, and there are chord progressions and figured bass examples relating to all harmonies that are introduced in Part 3.

For Part 2 (*Species Counterpoint*) and Part 4 (*Tonal Counterpoint*), some suggestions for exercises are included here, but these suggestions are far from complete treatments of these topics. It is assumed that students will find enough here for general purposes of theory study, and that more complex exercises can be developed by the teacher in class. Courses which require much more elaborate work in counterpoint are likely to be devoted solely to these subjects and to have their own textbooks.

Parts 5 and 6, on formal terms and instrumentation, are not covered by exercises in this section. The material on phrasing and form will make the most sense in the context of musical analysis, and this should certainly be done in any theory class. A good anthology will provide many examples of the forms and terms defined in Part 5. The description of transposition and the listings of instruments most used in classical contexts are provided in Part 6 for reference. These subjects are included in this book for students who may be looking at scores or composing stylistic pieces for a theory class. A more thorough study of instrumentation and orchestration will require a separate text.

Ideally, a student of theory will devote time to playing, singing, and listening to music. While the explanations in this book, along with the written exercises and keyboard progressions, will help musicians become much more conscious of the workings of the tonal language, ultimately, musical experience itself will be the best teacher.

EXERCISES FOR PART 1

(*pages* 1–7)

1. On staff paper, make a grand staff. In the treble clef write and label the following pitches: A, C♯, D, G, B♭, F. In the bass clef write and label E♭, A, G♯, C, F♯, B.

2. Draw an alto clef and place middle C on the center line. Write these pitches higher than middle C: G, D♯, A♭, F, and B♭. Then write the same pitches below middle C.
   Draw a tenor clef and write a middle C. Higher than middle C, write F, A, E♭, G♯, and B. Then write the same pitches lower than middle C.

3. Write the following pitches on the grand staff: c^1, D_1, f^2, A, g♯, e^1, "great C," b^2, d, g^1, F, e^3, b.

4. Write the following key signatures in the treble clef: A major, f minor, e minor, B major, D♭ major. Write these in the bass clef: d minor, E major, b♭ minor, c♯ minor.

5. What is the relative major of each key? d minor, c♯ minor, b♭ minor, b minor.
   What is the relative minor of each key? A♭ major, B major, B♭ major, G major.

6. Identify each key signature. Give both possible keys, major and minor.

7. On the grand staff (in both treble and bass clefs), write the flats in order; write the sharps in order.

8. Write scales in the clefs indicated. Do not include key signatures—mark each accidental. Mark half steps ˆ.
   Treble clef: E major; c♯ harmonic minor; f melodic minor up and down; F♯ major.
   Bass clef: b natural minor; A major; d melodic minor up and down; e harmonic minor.
   Alto clef: G major; c harmonic minor.
   Tenor clef: A♭ major; g melodic minor up and down.

9. Write the following minor scales, using key signatures, and add any necessary accidentals. Mark half steps ˆ.
   Treble clef: f♯ harmonic minor. Alto clef: a melodic minor, up and down. Bass clef: b♭ harmonic minor.

10. Write each mode in the clef indicated. Mark any half steps ˆ.
    Alto clef: Dorian, Aeolian; Treble clef: Lydian, Ionian; Bass clef: Mixolydian, Phrygian.

(*pages* 7–14)

1. Identify each interval, using abbreviations P = perfect, M = major, and m = minor. For example, 1) is a P4.

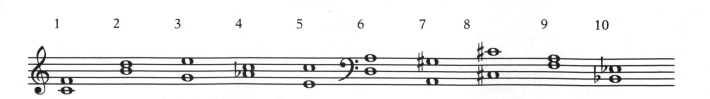

2. Identify each interval, using abbreviations P = perfect,
M = major, m = minor, d = diminished, + = augmented.

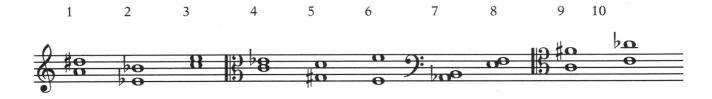

3. Write each interval (↑ means above the given note, ↓ means
below the given note).

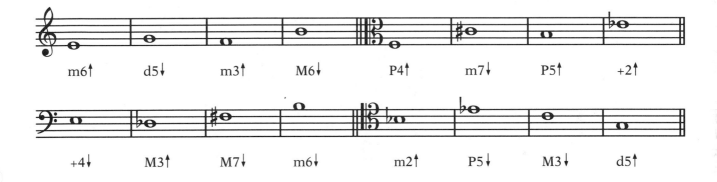

4. Identify each interval.

5. Write the intervals indicated.

6. Identify each interval. Note that there are key signatures.

7. In B major, name the dominant, mediant, leading tone, sub-dominant.

In F major, name the supertonic, subdominant, tonic, sub-mediant.

In d harmonic minor, name the dominant, leading tone, mediant, submediant.

In D major, name the dominant, leading tone, mediant, sub-mediant.

8. What is the meaning of each time signature? $\frac{3}{4}$, $\frac{6}{16}$, $\frac{5}{4}$, $\frac{2}{2}$, $\frac{9}{8}$

9. For each example below, correct the rhythmic notation to match the indicated time signature.

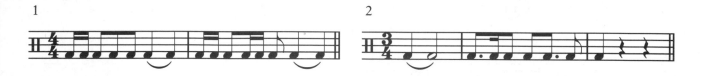

10. What is the difference between $\frac{3}{4}$ time and $\frac{6}{8}$ time?

How are the eighth notes grouped in $\frac{9}{8}$ time? in $\frac{12}{8}$ time?

11. For each example below, correct the rhythmic notation to match the indicated time signature. Add bar lines.

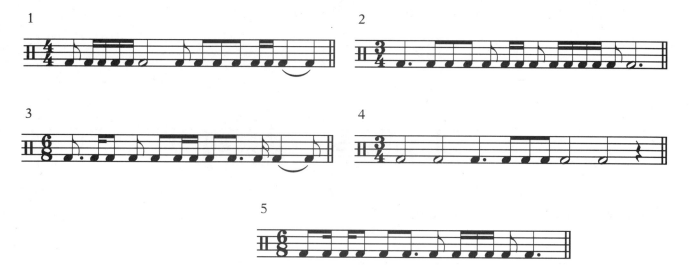

(*pages* 14–15)

1. Write the triads indicated. Do not use a key signature; supply all needed accidentals. E♭ major, g♯ minor, A major, b diminished, f minor, b♭ minor, c♯ diminished, D♭ major, E major, C augmented.

2. Identify the chord quality of each triad. Use abbreviations: M = major, m = minor, d = diminished, + = augmented.

3. Put each triad into root position, then identify the name and quality of each triad.

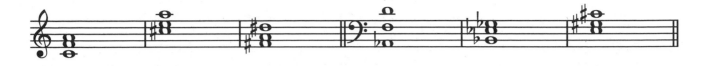

4. Write out all the triads of B♭ major. Label each triad with a Roman numeral, using large and small Roman numerals and o and + signs to indicate chord quality. Then do the same exercise in b♭ minor. Do not use key signatures—check all accidentals.

5. In the exercise above, which triads are the same in both major and minor modes?

6. Write triads in the keys and clefs indicated. Do not use key signatures; supply all necessary accidentals.
Treble clef: A major, I, IV, ii; e minor, III, ii°, V, VI; D♭ major, ii, V, iii, vii°; c minor, mediant, dominant.
Alto clef: B major, I, V, vi; D major, submediant, supertonic; F major, subdominant, submediant, leading tone.
Bass clef: f minor, III, ii°, V, VI; E major, mediant, dominant; c♯ minor, subdominant, leading tone, submediant.

7. Identify the chord quality of each triad. In major keys: tonic, dominant, supertonic, leading tone, subdominant, mediant, submediant. In minor keys: tonic, mediant, subdominant, leading tone, supertonic, submediant, dominant.

8. Identify each triad with a Roman numeral. Use upper and lower case, and o and + signs for chord quality.

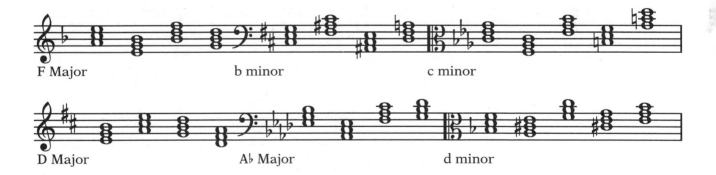

F Major   b minor   c minor

D Major   A♭ Major   d minor

EXERCISES FOR PART 2

1. Write melodies in whole notes, following the principles outlined under first species. Each of these can be used as a *cantus firmus* for counterpoint.

2. Write exercises in each of the five species, practicing both above and below a cantus firmus (CF). For all exercises, sing your line as you play the CF on the piano, or sing both parts in class. Always try to make your lines smooth and coherent. Each of the following CFs both begins and ends on the tonic. Each can therefore be used as an upper or lower part for exercises in any of the five species.

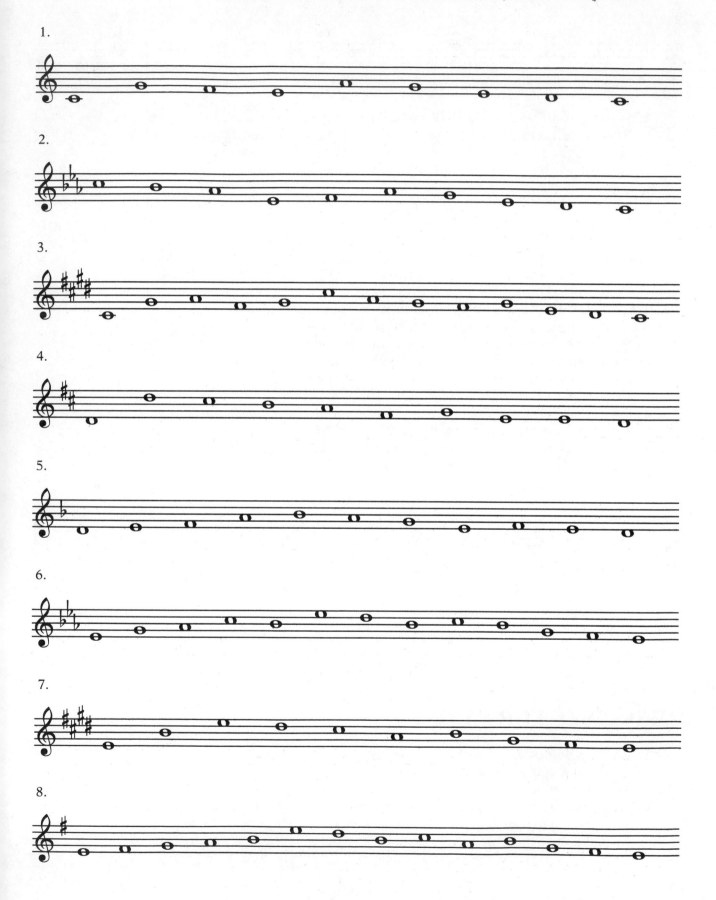

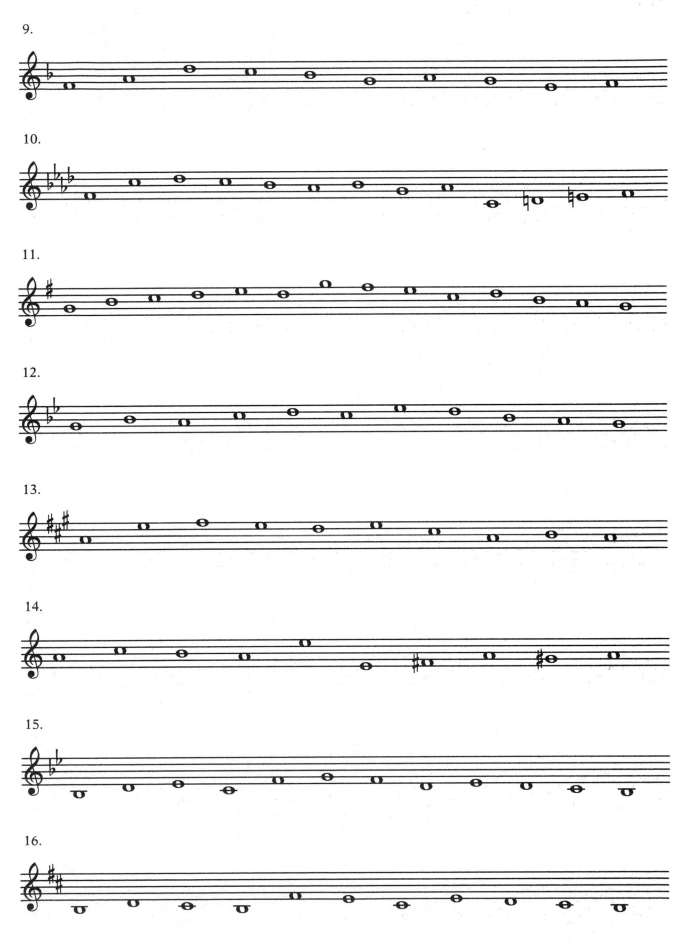

3. Take any of the two-voice motets by Roland de Lassus, play or sing the piece, and look for the following points: Within each voice, find the phrasing. The phrasing usually coincides with phrasing in the text. How is each phrase shaped in terms of its beginning, middle, and end? Is there a climax in the phrase? How does the rhythm tend to work within each phrase? What musical means are used to create cadences?

   Look for imitation between the two voices. If there is imitation, is it exact? How long does it go on? At what interval does one voice imitate the other? Is this intervalic distance maintained, or does it change at some point to a different interval? At what distance in time does the second voice imitate the first? What happens to the imitation as the cadence is approached.

   These questions will not have exactly the same answers in each motet. Therefore it is especially helpful to look at several different pieces for comparison.

4. Students who have mastered the species may wish to try a two-voice free counterpoint in the style of the Lassus motets. Use the following start to begin such a piece. This can be worked in imitation at the octave or fifth, and brought to a final or intermediate cadence. More phrases can be added. A familiar Latin text can be part of this project: *Dona nobis pacem, et in terra pax hominibus.*

EXERCISES FOR PART 3

(*pages* 33–38)

1. Write the key signature indicated, then write each progression in four voices, keeping common tones where possible: D major: I - V - I.   a minor: i - V - i.   E major: I - IV - V - I.   c minor: i - iv - V - i.

2. Label each chord with a Roman numeral. Play these progressions on the piano.

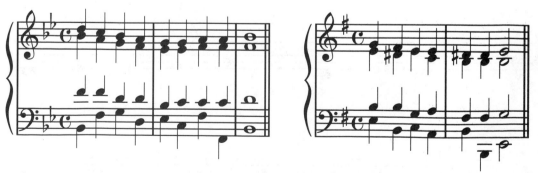

key?   key?

3. Write each progression, keeping common tones. Make sure to include a correct key signature for each:
   e minor: i - iv - V - i.   F major: I - vi - IV - V.   A♭ major: ii - V - I.
   b minor: i - V - i.   g minor: i - iv - V - i.   A major: I - vi - IV - ii - V.

4. Write these progressions, keeping common tones. Check accidentals and key signatures, watch for deceptive cadences and other exceptional situations. For each progression, label its *cadence type:* E♭ major: I - V - vi.   d minor: i - VI - V - i.
   c minor: ii° - V - i - iv - i.   f♯ minor: i - iv - V - VI.   G major: I - V - vi - iii - IV - ii - V - I.   B♭ major: I - vi - IV - V.

5. Use the bass lines to identify these root position progressions. Label with Roman numerals and add the upper parts.

*remember to use a
major V chord

6. Label each chord with a Roman numeral, and mark any passing tones (pt) or suspensions (sus) that you notice.

key:

7. Invent a progression in two mini-phrases. The first ends with a half cadence, the second ends with a full cadence. Use about 10 or 12 chords, all in root position. You may add some passing tones if your progression allows.

(pages 38–46)

1. For each specified key, write each chord in the inversion indicated. Do not worry about voice leading between chords: A♭ major: I⁶, V⁶, ii, I$^6_4$, vii°⁶, IV$^6_4$.   b minor: V⁶, i⁶, ii°⁶, VI, i$^6_4$, vii°⁶.

2. Analyze the following progression, labeling each chord. Make sure to include inversions in your labeling.

3. Write each progression, being careful about ii⁶: f minor: i - ii°⁶ - V - VI.   B major: I - ii⁶ - V - I⁶ - IV - V - I.

4. Derive each progression from the bass line, adding missing Roman numerals. Inverted chords are already labeled. Write out the progressions in four voices.

5. Harmonize this fragment in two ways, using only the chords learned so far. Label all chords with Roman numerals.

6. Label each chord with a Roman numeral. Mark any neighbor tones (nt) or passing tones (pt).

7. Write these progressions in four voices. For each example include a key signature, meter, and bar lines.

a minor: i - VI - iv - V - i.   Bb major: I - ii⁶ - I⁶₄ - V - I.   c minor:
i - vii°⁶ - i⁶.   f# minor: i - ii°⁶ - V - VI.
E major: I - IV⁶ - V⁶ - I.   d minor: ii°⁶ - V - i⁶.   Eb major: I - vi - IV -
I⁶₄ - V - I.   b minor: i - iv⁶ - V.

8. Invent an example for each of the following six-four chord types:
   cadential I⁶₄, passing I⁶₄, neighbor (pedal) IV⁶₄.

9. Label Roman numerals and nonharmonic tones in the phrases
   below. Label the cadence type at each fermata.

key:

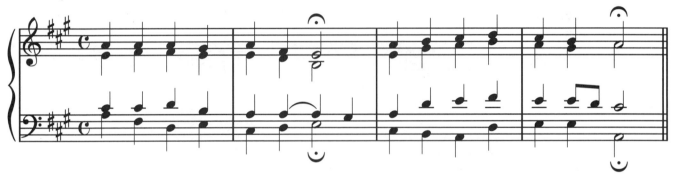

key:

(*pages* 46–51)

1. Write each dominant 7th chord and resolution in the key and inver-
   sion specified. Use key signatures.
   F major: V-⁷ - I.   e minor V⁶₅ - i.   B major: V⁴₃ - I.   d minor: V⁴₂ - i⁶.
   Eb major: V-⁷ - vi.   a minor: V⁴₃ -i⁶.   c minor: V-⁷ - VI.   G major
   V⁴₂ - I⁶.   D major: V⁴₃ - I⁶.   f minor: V⁴₃ - i.   Bb major: V-⁷ - I.
   f# minor: V⁴₃ - i.

2. Identify the key and inversion of each V-⁷ chord below. Resolve to I
   or I⁶.

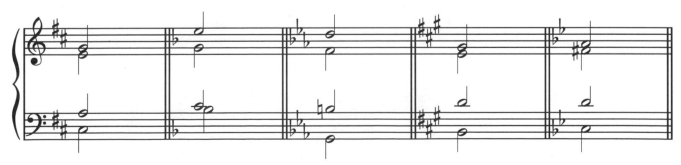

3. Write each progression in four voices, including key and time signatures: d minor: i - ii°^{6} - V-^{7} - VI.   B♭ major: I - V - V$^4_2$ - I^6 - I$^6_4$ - V-^{7} - I.

4. Label each bass line with Roman numerals, then write out each progression in four voices.

5. Analyze:

key:

6. Write in four voices: A major: I - ii$^6_5$ - V-^{7} - I.   e minor: i - VI - ii°$^6_5$ - V$^4_2$ - i^6. Include key and time signatures.

7. Realize this figured bass in four voices. Label all chords.

8. Harmonize this tune in chorale style. Use ii⁶₅ in the final
cadence pattern.

(*pages* 51–55)

1. Write each progression in four voices. Include key signature,
meter, and bar lines: f minor: i - V$^4_2$/iv - iv⁶.   G major: I - vi -
V⁶₅/V - V.   A major: I - vi - V$^4_2$/ii - ii⁶ - V-⁷ - I.   d minor: i - ii°⁶ -
V⁶₅/V - V-⁷ - VI.

2. Realize in four voices. Label all chords.

3. Identify each triad in the indicated key. Watch for both major
and minor mode triads and secondary dominants.

F: e: D:

4. Write triads in the keys indicated: B major: V/V; vi; VI; ii°.
c♯ minor: V/iv; III; V/V.   A major: iv, V/ii; V/iii.

5. Copy this bar, and continue
the progression to a tonicization of D major. Use the vi
chord (last chord) to pivot
toward D. In D, this chord will
function as ii; bracket the ii
and all the chords that follow
it over a V label. Now copy
this bar again, and this time
tonicize e minor. Again use the
vi chord to pivot. Copy the
starting bar again, and now go
to C major; start again and go
to b minor. Always use the vi
chord as the pivot, and bracket
each tonicization over a Roman numeral label. Try to make a

G: I   V   I   *vi*

(pivot)

convincing cadence in your tonicized key. Use melodic line and metric placement to help establish the cadence point.

6. Harmonize the following familiar tunes. Write out in four voices, with the given tune as the soprano. Label with Roman numerals. Play your chords on the piano, listening carefully to the bass. Try to find harmonies that sound typical and natural for these tunes. Don't seek unusual solutions; the purpose of this exercise is to become conscious of familiar patterns in a familiar context.

    a) You may wish to use a secondary dominant on the second beat of measure 4.

    b) In this tune, the pickup notes and the last four notes are often played in octaves, with no harmony.

7. Harmonize these two chorale tunes. You may want to look up Bach's harmonizations.

WERDE MUNTER, MEIN GEMÜTE

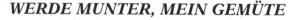

ALLE MENSCHEN MÜSSEN STERBEN

(*pages* 56–62)

1. Write in four voices: B♭: vii°7 - I.   f♯ minor: vii°6/5 - i6.   A♭ major: vii°7 - I.   c♯ minor: vii°6/5 -i6.   e minor: vii°4/3 - i6.

2. Use the spelling to identify each diminished 7th chord below. Label and resolve.

3. Write a diminished 7th chord in which B is the root; identify the key and resolve. Now respell the chord, making B the third; identify the key and resolve. Respell again, with B as the fifth. Identify the key and resolve. Repeat this exercise, using c♯ as the root, the third, and the fifth of the diminished 7th chords. Identify each key and resolve each chord.

4. Write each progression in four voices. Use key signatures: A major: vii°7/vi - vi.   d minor: V6/5/V - V.   f minor: iv6 - V.   B♭ major: V4/2 - I6. c♯ minor: vii°6/5 - i6.   G major: vii°4/3 /ii - ii6.   e minor: V4/2 /iv - iv6.   D♭ major: vii°7/V - V.

5. Write each progression in four voices. Supply key signatures, meter, and bar lines:
C major: V - I - vii°7/ii - ii - ii6 - I6/4 - V-7 - vi.   b minor: i - vii°6 - i6 - i - VI - i6/4 - ii°6/5 - V-7 - i.

6. Realize each figured bass below in four voices. Label all chords.

7. Analyze with Roman numerals, labeling nonharmonic tones. This progression tonicizes a new key at the end. Use a bracket to label chords in the new key.

8. Write each progression in four voices. Watch for borrowed chords! G major: I - ♭VI - V⁶₅/V - V-⁷ - I.   A major: I - V⁴₃ - I⁶ - ii°⁶ - V.   E major: I - V⁴₂/IV - IV⁶ - iv⁶ - I⁶₄ - V-⁷ - I.   b minor: i - IV⁶ - V⁶ - i - ii°⁶ - i⁶₄ - V-⁷ - I.

9. Write the Neapolitan 6th in each key (use key signatures). Resolve to V. A♭ major, c♯ minor, E major, b minor, D major.

10. Write each progression. Include key and time signatures. E♭ major: I - ♭II⁶ - V-⁷ - I.   f♯ minor: i - vii°⁶ - i⁶ - ♭II⁶ - i⁶₄ - V-⁷ - VI.   G major: I - V - V⁴₂ - I⁶ - ♭II⁶ - I⁶₄ - V⁶₅/V - V.

11. Write the key signature and chord specified. Resolve each chord to V: e minor: Fr⁺⁶.   B♭ major: ♭II⁶.   A major: It⁺⁶. b minor: Gr⁺⁶ - i⁶₄.   E major: ♭II⁶ - I⁶₄.   d minor: It⁺⁶. G major: Gr⁺⁶ - I⁶₄.   f♯ minor: Fr⁺⁶ - i⁶₄.   g minor: vii°⁷/V.

12. Assume that this entire exercise is in D major. Label each chord with a Roman numeral. Watch for borrowed chords, secondary dominant and diminished chords, Neapolitans, and augmented sixth chords.

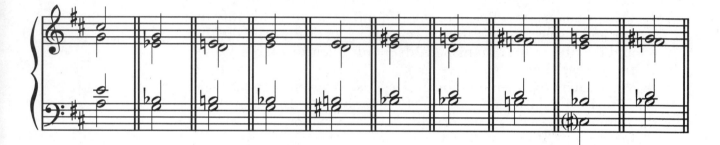

13. Write these progressions in four voices. These use common tone diminished 7th chords—watch spelling!
F major: I - vii°⁶ - ♯ii°⁷ - I⁶ - IV - vii°⁷/V - V - I.   G major: I - vii°⁷/vi - vi - ♯vi°⁷ - V⁶₅ - V-⁷ - I.   B♭ major: I - ♯vi°₅ - V⁴₃ - ♯vi°⁷ - V⁶₅ - I - V. D♭ major: I⁶ - ♯ii°⁷ - I⁶ - IV - vii°♭⁷/V - V - I - ♯ii°⁴₂ - I.

14. Invent progressions of four to eight chords each, with the following characteristics: D major, uses a ♭II⁶.   g minor, uses a Gr⁺⁶ and has a deceptive cadence.   E major, uses ♯vi°⁷ and V⁴₂/IV. f♯ minor, uses Fr⁺⁶ and ♭II⁶.

(*pages* 63–65)

1. In the common practice period, a piece that begins in a major key is likely to modulate to the dominant. What will the goal of modulation be if a piece begins in A major? In D-flat major? In B major? In E-flat major? In F-sharp major?

   Pieces in minor keys are likely to move to the relative major. What is the likely goal of modulation if a piece begins in f minor? in c-sharp minor? in b-flat minor? in e minor? in f-sharp minor?

   Pieces in minor sometimes modulate to the minor dominant. Name the minor dominant of d minor; b minor; a minor.

2. Name all the *closely related keys* of A-flat major; b minor; E major; g-sharp minor; F major.

3. Begin in the key of D major. Establish the key, then make a modulation to A major. Use melodic line and metric placement as well as harmony to make the modulation convincing. Label all chords with Roman numerals, and make sure to label the pivot chord clearly. Following the same directions, begin in F major, modulate to d minor. Begin in G major, modulate to a minor.

4. Following the directions given for number 3 above, begin in c minor and modulate to E-flat major. Begin in a minor and modulate to e minor. Begin in b minor and modulate to G major.

5. Write a 16-bar tune in a major key that follows this harmonic outline: Begin on I and come to a full cadence in measure 4; in measures 5–8 tonicize V, ending with a full cadence on V; in measures 9–12 "untonicize" V, so that you can end in measure 12 with V sounding like a half cadence (as opposed to a full cadence); return to I with a full cadence in measure 16. Make sure that the tune itself is coherent, graceful, and pleasing. Harmonize in four voices, label all chords.

6. In a minor key write a 16-bar tune that follows this harmonic outline: Begin on i and go to a full cadence in measure 4; in measures 5–8, tonicize III, ending with a full cadence on III; in measures 9–12 come back to the original tonic, ending in measure 12 on a half cadence; make measures 13–16 a variation of measures 1–4, ending with a full cadence. Harmonize your tune in four voices, and label all chords with Roman numerals.

SUGGESTED PROJECTS FOR PART 4

Students who have progressed through all the earlier material in this book will have a good knowledge of harmony. The following ideas for projects assume such a background, and are aimed at somewhat advanced students.

1. Write upper-part counterpoints for each of these Bach figured basses. Following the harmony outlined in the figures, first write upper parts in steady quarters (except at the cadences). Then, start again, and write counterpoints in steady eighths. These are taken from the chorale melodies with figured bass.

ERMUNTRE DICH, MEIN SCHWACHER GEIST

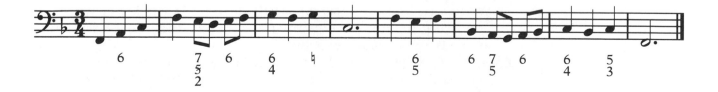

NUR MEIN JESUS IST MEIN LEBEN

2. Harmonize these two chorale tunes by Bach. Then write lower-part counterpoints, first in quarters, then in eighths. You might wish to look up the several chorale versions of both tunes made by Bach himself.

O GOTT, DU FROMMER GOTT

JESU, MEINE FREUDE

3. Create counterpoints to these tunes that are invertible at the octave (or fifteenth). Write out both versions of each.

4. Create a simple round, staying essentially on the tonic. Then create a round that has some pre-dominant and dominant harmony, in addition to I. Write out both rounds through the completion of the second voice, and check your harmony. Perform these in class.

5. Write a two-voice canon at the fifth. Start in the lower voice, and bring the upper voice in after one bar. Include a harmonic analysis underneath your work.

6. Students who can write two-voice invertible counterpoint and canons are ready to go on to contrapuntal pieces in two voices (modeled on Bach *Inventions,* for example), and to writing in three and four voices. The techniques developed here will serve for more complex harmonic structures in longer pieces, and for more extended contrapuntal works, such as fugues and chorale preludes. These projects can be designed by the teacher and students.